★ Walking St. Augustine

CITY GATES, LOOKING SOUTH, ST. AUGUSTINE, FLA.

UNIVERSITY PRESS OF FLORIDA

Florida A&M University, Tallahassee
Florida Atlantic University, Boca Raton
Florida Gulf Coast University, Ft. Myers
Florida International University, Miami
Florida State University, Tallahassee
New College of Florida, Sarasota
University of Central Florida, Orlando
University of Florida, Gainesville
University of North Florida, Jacksonville
University of South Florida, Tampa
University of West Florida, Pensacola

Walking
St. Augustine

❖ An Illustrated Guide
❖ and Pocket History
❖ to America's Oldest City

ELSBETH "BUFF" GORDON

University Press of Florida

Gainesville · Tallahassee · Tampa · Boca Raton

Pensacola · Orlando · Miami · Jacksonville · Ft. Myers · Sarasota

VIVA FLORIDA 500.
1513-2013

A Florida Quincentennial Book

Publication of this book is made possible by the generosity of University of Florida Historic St. Augustine, Inc., and the St. Augustine Foundation, Inc.

Printed in Korea on acid-free paper

This book may be available in an electronic edition.

23 22 21 20 19 18   8 7 6 5 4 3

Library of Congress Control Number: 2014951464
ISBN 978-0-8130-6083-5

The University Press of Florida is the scholarly publishing agency for the State University System of Florida, comprising Florida A&M University, Florida Atlantic University, Florida Gulf Coast University, Florida International University, Florida State University, New College of Florida, University of Central Florida, University of Florida, University of North Florida, University of South Florida, and University of West Florida.

University Press of Florida
15 Northwest 15th Street
Gainesville, FL 32611-2079
http://upress.ufl.edu

To the time-honored Oldest City

Full swelled the sail before the driving wind,
Till the stout pilot turned his prow to land,
Where peered, mid orange groves & Citron boughs,
The little city of St. Augustine.

There liest thou, little city of the deep,
And always hearest the unceasing sound
By day and night, in summer and in frost,
The roar of waters on thy coral shore.

RALPH WALDO EMERSON, 1827

Contents

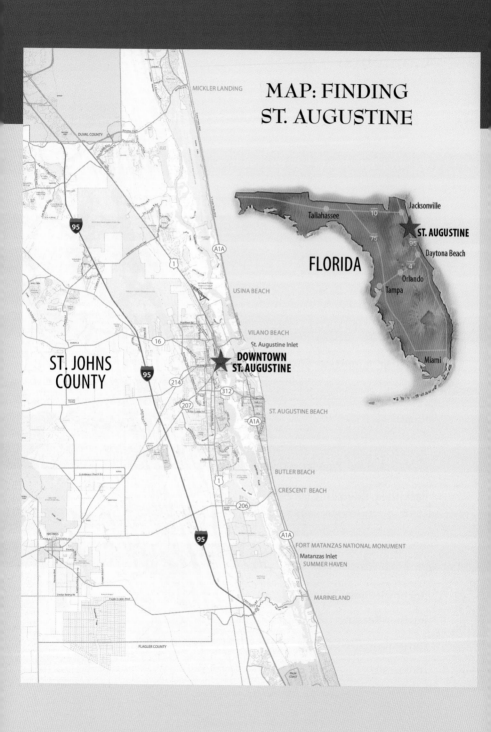

MAP: FINDING ST. AUGUSTINE

MICKLER LANDING

DUVAL COUNTY

95

1

A1A

USINA BEACH

VILANO BEACH

St. Augustine Inlet

DOWNTOWN ST. AUGUSTINE

ST. AUGUSTINE BEACH

BUTLER BEACH

CRESCENT BEACH

206

FORT MATANZAS NATIONAL MONUMENT

Matanzas Inlet
SUMMER HAVEN

MARINELAND

PALM COAST

ST. JOHNS COUNTY

95

16

214

312

207

1

A1A

FLAGLER COUNTY

Jacksonville

Tallahassee

10

75

FLORIDA

4

Orlando

Tampa

95

ST. AUGUSTINE

Daytona Beach

Miami

Introduction
How to Use This Guide

St. Augustine was 224 years old when George Washington became president of the United States in 1789. At the city's heart today is the colonial walled town that was once, long ago, defended by barricades fashioned from earth, cactus, wood, and stone. The original walls are gone, but what they guarded is now an American shrine—the Oldest European City in the United States.

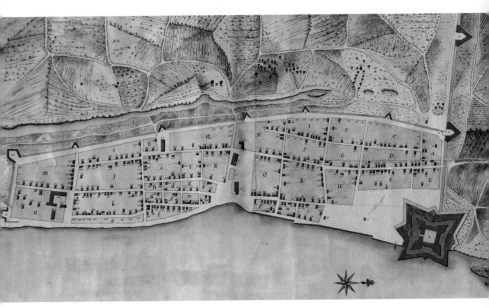

This guidebook takes you there! It will open doors to the colonists' houses then and now and to five centuries of events and untold personal stories that illustrate American history. As you walk this small intimate city of the centuries, the book's guided tours will lead you to intriguing discoveries about the people who have settled in the historic seacoast town since the sixteenth century.

Twenty-first-century St. Augustine is expanding around the colonial walled town to the north, west, and south, leaving its historic center intact. To the east is water: a tidal river and an ocean, rolling surf and sand beaches. In 2013, *National Geographic Traveler* chose St. Augustine as one of "20 must-see places and best trips in the world."

What You Will Discover

Part 1 introduces you to St. Augustine's beginnings. Your discoveries start in section 1, "Busting the Myth." In section 2, "The Spanish Landing, 1565," witness the day-by-day drama of the city's founding and the move to Anastasia Island forced by the flaming arrows of Indian retaliation. Learn why the settlers leave the island and rebuild their town back on the mainland in 1572–73.

In section 3, "Discovering St. Augustine in Ancient Maps," rare, centuries-old maps reveal what Spanish and British St. Augustine looked like from 1565 to 1784.

Section 4 is a time line. It offers you a quick and easy way to learn the city's history and compare it with other places in the United States and the world.

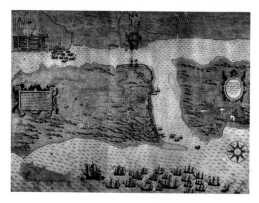

Part 2, "St. Augustine, Street by Street,"
divides the colonial walled town into three
historic walking-tour areas: "The Plaza";
"South of the Plaza"; and "North of the
Plaza." Each tour area has self-guided walks
accompanied by street maps marked with
places and houses to see. Start with any tour area. Walk any part
of any tour that interests you and is convenient with your plans—
the maps are easy to follow. All walking tours start and end near
the Plaza that is the historic center of St. Augustine. No tour is far
from drinks or food.

House histories, myths, legends, and intimate personal stories
are carefully researched—they are the real story of our nation's
oldest city. Occasional text boxes and sidebars will alert you to
special information that is worth knowing. Looking for unusual
people stories? Authentic history? Spanish, British, and early-
American-period genealogies? Climate-friendly house ideas?
An escape into another lifetime? This guide to St. Augustine is a
treasure trove.

Each walking area has special characteristics related to its
historical past and the people who lived there—and what is
preserved for us to see. For example, as you tour the centuries-old
Plaza (section 5), you will witness the formation of the sixteenth-
century town, its public square, parish church, and governor's
house in the stories about the buildings facing today's Plaza.

At the westernmost end of the Plaza Walk, look upward at the towers of Henry Flagler's three 1800s Spanish Renaissance Revival–style resort hotels—Hotel Ponce de Leon, Hotel Alcazar, and Hotel Cordova—now preserved with stunning new uses as Flagler College, Lightner Museum and City of St. Augustine offices and meeting rooms, and Casa Monica Hotel. They are immediately outside the former walls of the colonial town, but their Gilded Age arts and modern energies transform the colonial Plaza and are part of the Plaza story.

Section 6, "South of the Plaza Tours," has two guided walks into the city's earliest residential area—the only place in the continental United States where residents today go about their daily lives and businesses in streets that have been continuously used since 1572. Here you will find the greatest number of the city's extant colonial house museums. It is also rich with U.S. territorial- and Victorian-period houses, bed-and-breakfast inns, a former Spanish monastery, a National Cemetery, and a waterfront promenade with winter cottages of the post–Civil War residents.

Section 7, "North of the Plaza Tour," takes you to the reconstructed area to explore colonial houses saved from bulldozers and given new life. As you walk St. George, Treasury, Spanish, Cuna, Hypolita, and Charlotte Streets with this guidebook's recently discovered stories, you will meet the people whose lives are stamped in the centuries-old timbers and stones. Their houses once again serve as shops, taverns, bakeries, eateries, and residences, like

they did in colonial times. "North of the Plaza Tour" also includes the Colonial Quarter Living History Museum, a two-acre interactive attraction that brings to life Spanish and British colonial history. This tour also leads you to old cemeteries and the Castillo de San Marcos, which saved the city from two British sieges and is the oldest stone fort in the continental United States.

Part 3, "St. Augustine Forever," is a twenty-first-century view of residents. How do people living and working in a historic city preserve the Spanish patina and tell the story of diversity? How do their houses and businesses reflect the Oldest City's colonial image, and how will its history be remembered? What makes their city look and feel like no other historic city in the United States? Sections 8 and 9 serve up an answer or two in the heritage recipes, in craftsmen and innkeepers at work, and in reenactors enlivening the real  life dramas of past centuries. Buildings marked with an asterisk (*) in this guide's walks are owned by the State of Florida and managed by University of Florida Historic St. Augustine, Inc.

At the Visitor Information Center (VIC), north of the City Gate and adjacent to the Visitors Parking Garage, there are restrooms and a gift shop, information about attractions, lodging, and transportation, and a gallery with changing exhibits related to St. Augustine's cultural history.

Places to Visit Outside the Walled Town

Anastasia Island

Cross the Bridge of Lions east of the Plaza to visit the fifteen-mile-long Anastasia Island. The white sand beaches, popular amphitheater, and historic attractions require transportation and are not included in this guidebook's walks. That said, the island's must-see places are St. Augustine Historic Lighthouse and Museum, 1876, with its keeper's house and underwater treasures pulled from the deep; St. Augustine Alligator Farm and Zoological Park, 1893, including its new Crocodile Crossing Zipline; and Fort Matanzas, 1742, near the island's southern tip. Across Matanzas Inlet is Marineland, 1938, the world's first ocean-arium, and underwater film studio, now Marineland Dolphin Adventure.

Fort Mose

Also requiring transportation is Fort Mose—Gracia Real de Santa Teresa de Mose—two miles north of Castillo de San Marcos. Fort Mose, the nation's first legally free black settlement, was built in 1738 as a defensive fort-village that granted refuge to slaves escaping from English plantations. Striking back, the English destroyed the fort in 1740. Rebuilt close to the first site in 1752, it is today an archaeological site. Fort Mose Historic State Park has a boardwalk, a history museum, and an exciting annual reenactment of the 1740 battle known as Bloody Mose. The site is designated a National Historic Landmark.

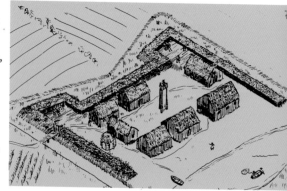

Fort Matanzas, 1742

Boat service and tours to Fort Matanzas are provided by the National Park Service. The small coquina fort stands on Rattlesnake Island overlooking Matanzas Inlet. It was built to defend the ocean inlet and the river that were the back door to the Spanish capital. Engineer Pedro Ruiz de Olano had to sink wood pilings in the soft sand to support the little fort's coquina construction. Even so, by 1820 it was badly cracked. Restored just in time, the fort was declared a National Monument in 1924. Step into the tiny living space that was the Spanish soldiers' lonely home as they kept their vigil by the cannon under the red-and-white Cross of Burgundy Spanish flag.

Fountain of Youth Archaeological Park

Privately owned, the park is about a mile north of the Castillo de San Marcos. It is the archaeological site of the 1565 encampment of Pedro Menéndez de Avilés. In the park's grounds there are Christian Indian burials and the remains of Chief Seloy's sixteenth-century Indian village. Nombre de Dios, the Franciscan mission, might have been established here in 1587. There is also evidence of prehistoric Indian occupation. Pathways with interpretive panels lead to reconstructed Timucua houses, a mission church, a watchtower, and a chalupa (shallop) boatyard—and to a drink from the park's Fountain of Youth to revive you. Open to the public; tickets can be purchased on-site.

Mission Nombre de Dios

This peaceful spiritual place belongs to the Catholic Diocese of St. Augustine—historically it was part of the Indian village of the Franciscan mission, Nombre de Dios. A tall steel cross overlooks the ocean inlet through which the Spanish arrived in 1565. Near the cross, archaeologists are excavating what is believed to be a seventeenth-century mission church.

On the mission grounds is the 1918 Shrine of Nuestra Señora de la Leche (Our Nursing Mother), a reconstruction of a seventeenth-century shrine, open daily to visitors. There is also a museum dedicated to the centuries of Catholic history in St. Augustine.

Lincolnville

West of Maria Sanchez Creek and Cordova Street, beyond the colonial walled town, is Lincolnville, a 45-block area that is a post–Civil War freedmen settlement and Victorian-era residential neighborhood. It is the center of today's African American community in St. Augustine, and of an active restoration program and a civil rights museum. Lincolnville is a National Register Historic District.

PART I

❖
❖
❖ St. Augustine!
Before Jamestown,
Before Plymouth

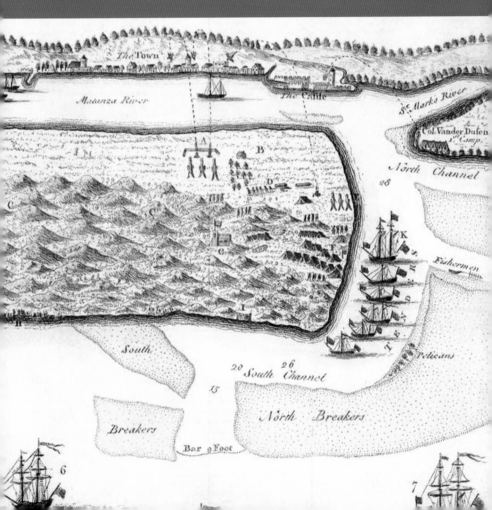

1

Busting the Myth

You are in the Plaza; it is 1586. Francis Drake's English soldiers are attacking the city. At the western end of the Plaza, they set the Spanish governor's house on fire; at the eastern end of the Plaza near the harbor, they pillage and burn the parish church. Then they torch the residential neighborhood to the south, and as they leave, they set fire to the wood fort to the north. The embers glow as Drake sails away.

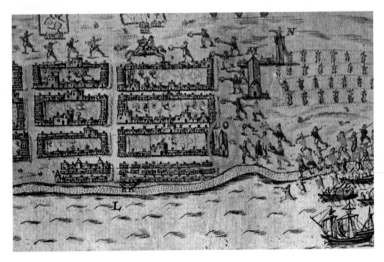

St. Augustine's First Folk Hero

In the cornfield west of the city, the killing of Captain Anthony Powell takes place during Drake's raid in 1586. Powell is one of Sir Francis Drake's best captains and a kinsman. The Spanish hero is Juan Ramírez de Contreras, soldier, interpreter, Indian trader, and seller of Indian corn. At great danger to himself, he volunteers to entice the mounted English captain to give chase, separating him from his troops. Wounded by Powell's lance, Ramírez rises up and slays the enemy. This death scene was drawn by Baptista Boazio on the map that depicts Drake's raid. Boazio shows Powell kneeling on the ground, hands raised, his riderless horse rearing as the Spaniard's sword delivers the mortal blow.

As Americans do today after floods or fires, the Spanish residents rebuilt their city. Four decades before Jamestown was founded and five decades before Plymouth, St. Augustine was constructed and reconstructed. Astonishingly, there are people today who still believe that the first European settlements in the United States were in Virginia or Massachusetts.

"Florida, sir, is not worth buying. It is a land of swamps, of quagmires, of frogs and alligators and mosquitoes! A man, sir, would not immigrate into Florida. No sir! No man would immigrate into Florida—no, not from hell itself!" John Randolph, Virginia's delegate to the U.S. Congress in 1821, is widely quoted arguing that the United States should not acquire Florida. Yet since 1565 people from many places in the world had continued to immigrate to St. Augustine. Before the ink dried on the 1819

Adams-Onís Treaty that made Florida a U.S. territory, Americans left states to the north, and with wagons piled high with family and possessions, they, too, rolled into the old Spanish capital.

What Is Special about St. Augustine?

St. Augustine was first in many things the nation holds dear. It was the first permanent colonial capital and seat of government. The first Thanksgiving in the United States occurred at the Spanish landing site in 1565 (see "The Spanish Landing, 1565"), and the 1572–73 town plan was the first in North America. Residents built the first Franciscan monastery, Indian mission, governor's house, and hospital, and they planted the first orange groves and established the first cattle ranches. St. Augustine was first to recognize legal female property ownership, and first to grant amnesty to enslaved Africans (1693) and establish a legal black settlement (1738). Its sixteenth-century Christian parish still exists, and descendants of the first families still live in the city.

Indian Village and Mission Nombre de Dios

In the Indian pueblo Nombre de Dios, north of the fort, Alonso Gregorio de Escobedo began his assignment in 1587 as the first resident friar of what was to become the nation's oldest, longest lasting Franciscan mission. A drawing of the pueblo and mission buildings was presented by Lt. Hernando de Mestas to the king of Spain in 1594. Mestas noted that the Indian pueblo was one thousand paces from the fort. His 1594 diagram is redrawn here to show how the Catholic religious buildings in A (church, convent, kitchen) stood near the traditional Indian buildings in B, (the chief's council house, chief's residence, and two raised granaries topped with crosses). The chief was responsible for supplying the fort with corn. All buildings appear to be wood and thatch.

St. Augustine's Building Materials: Wood, Tabby, Coquina

During the sixteenth and seventeenth centuries, St. Augustine was
a fortified military town, a presidio
constructed mostly with wood, the
region's most plentiful material.
No wood buildings constructed
before 1702 survive. The buildings
destroyed by Sir Francis Drake in
1586 were later rebuilt but were
burned again by Carolina's Col.
James Moore in 1702. Some of the
timber and planked buildings live
on in documents and archaeological
findings to tell us where they stood
and what they looked like.

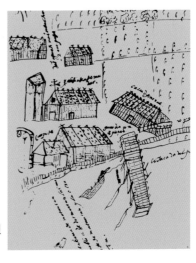

At the end of the seventeenth century, a few residents were
building masonry buildings using tabby, coquina blocks, and a
combination of tabby and coquina rubble. The coquina walls of
the 1672 Castillo de San Marcos were proving to be the future, im-
pervious to rot, termites, and fire. In the 1690s, coquina from the
royal quarry on Anastasia Island was made available to residents

who could afford it. After
the 1702 British siege in
which all of wooden St.
Augustine was burned,
coquina blocks were used
for official buildings and
the better houses, and by
the mid-1700s, many more
house walls had taken
shape with coquina blocks
covered with protective
coats of white stucco.

What Are Archaeological Findings?

Archaeology is the study of past human cultures and behavior. Colonial archaeological findings include pottery, tools, bones, food remains, fabrics, buttons, weapons, and construction materials. Scientifically examined, these artifacts can suggest to archaeologists what colonists built, ate, wore, manufactured, and imported, and how and when buildings were constructed and used. The City of St. Augustine employs an archaeologist to examine construction sites and protect archaeological findings. There is always an air of expectation in the Ancient City that a new discovery is about to happen. You are welcome to stop by archaeological sites and ask questions.

❖   ❖   ❖

What Is Tabby?

Tabby is a concrete. It was made in colonial times by hand-mixing sand, water, and quicklime (made by burning oyster shells) and adding an aggregate of oyster shells or coquina rubble or gravel. Tabby walls were fabricated in layers. The sand-lime-water-shell mixture was poured and tamped into wood forms, and after the first layer hardened, the wood form was removed and placed on top to receive the next poured layer. The process continued until the desired wall height was reached. Tabby floors had a similar mixture except for a smaller aggregate.

❖   ❖   ❖

What Is Coquina?

Coquina is the native Florida rock or shell-stone quarried on Anastasia Island that is special to St. Augustine architecture. It is composed of the Donax and other clamshells cemented together by calcium carbonate over long periods of geological time, so well cemented as to appear to be one solid stone. Coquina was discovered in 1586 but was not used until 1672, when the Spanish king gave permission and funds to build a stone castillo to replace the rotting wood forts. Coquina slabs were cut at the royal quarry, rafted across the river, hewn into building blocks, and mortared with oyster-shell lime. The stone Castillo de San Marcos was never defeated; the coquina walls never splintered or burned—they absorbed enemy cannonballs.

Why Are St. Augustine's Streets Narrow?

On your tours, notice how the coquina houses built up to the
street edge create shade for pedestrians in the city's subtropical
climate. Historically this also conserved most of each lot for the
kitchen gardens, water wells, and livestock that supplemented
a family's military pay. Narrow streets were also a means of
defense.

Colonial St. Augustine Architecture

Colonial architecture uniquely reflects the city's cultural diversity
under Spanish and British governments as well as the oceanfront
site, the climate, the materials from the sea, and the city's history
and defensive concerns.

Early Spanish houses were generally entered through a side
fence or wall that led into a south-facing patio or a loggia protected from cold north winds. The first masonry houses com-
monly had flat roofs and water-
spouts to divert rainwater away
from walls. Large window openings
were protected by wood grilles
(*rejas*) and interior shutters. If
there was a second story, it might
have a covered wood balcony—an
indoor-outdoor room where families collected in the cool of evening.
A 1740s resident described the
architectural style as being "in the
style of the country."

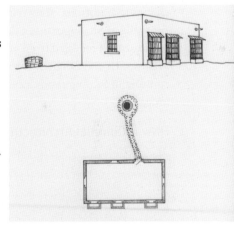

To these Spanish house tradi-
tions, the arriving British added a few of their own that reflect
their mother country's colder climate, or adaptations made in
their tropical Caribbean plantations. Wood second stories with
pitched gables and British carpentry were added to Spanish-built
stone first stories. British-style chimneys and fireplaces replaced

Spanish charcoal braziers. Glazed
window sashes became common.
The British, however, adopted
Spanish covered balconies, loggias,
enclosed kitchen gardens, and residential side entrances. Examples of
colonial houses that combine these
Spanish and British traditions still
stand.

The Old House
on St. Francis Street,
St. Augustine, Fla.

What Is Unique about St. Augustine's Diversity?

St. Augustine is the only city in the United States that has been
continuously inhabited since the sixteenth century. Its Old World
patina and human-scaled street plan and buildings have been
nurtured over centuries by people from many different cultures
and ethnic backgrounds living under three different national governments. Never very rich, the multicultural colonists adapted to
changing traditions. They reused buildings and materials: touch
the walls of St. Augustine's Cathedral—in them are the old coquina stones recycled from earlier Spanish and English churches.
Walk south and north of the sixteenth-century Plaza and find
comfort in St. Augustine's cultural diversity, its humanness and
longevity.

How Is Colonial Architecture Discovered?

Although St. Augustine's buildings may be described in historical
documents such as eyewitness descriptions or official reports, these
documents are not always accurate, complete, or up-to-date. They were
written by people with differing viewpoints, motives, and biases, and
the translations of Spanish documents can vary, adding more confu-
sion. Therefore, it is important that house floor plans and construction
methods and materials be unearthed in controlled excavations and
that the evidence be examined and dated by professionals trained in
archaeology, history, and architecture.

Who Were the Colonists?

St. Augustine's colonial population was uniquely diverse compared to other colonial societies in North America. Early in the First Spanish Period, residents came from various regions of Spain and Africa, different American Indian tribes, Portugal, Cuba, Mexico, the Canary Islands, France, Germany, England, and Ireland. During the British and the Second Spanish Periods, more residents came from England, Scotland, Ireland, Africa, Spain, Cuba, the Canaries, Minorca, Greece, Italy, Switzerland, and the Anglo-American colonies north of Florida. In all periods, there were people of mixed races as more children were born in St. Augustine of Spanish, Indian, African, and British unions. Free and enslaved people of African heritage were present from the beginning, including Juan Diego de Amaya, who was born in 1523 in the West African kingdom of Kabbu Mandinka and was educated in Lisbon, Portugal.

❖　❖　❖

Changes in Government

St. Augustine had four changes in government before Florida became a state in 1845. Government House served as the residence and office of the Spanish and British governors and as the courthouse and offices of the territorial government. Remember these historical periods as you walk the city streets:

First Spanish Period: 1565–1763
British Period: 1763–1783 (1784 by the time the British left and the
    Spanish arrived)
Second Spanish Period: 1783–1821
U.S. Territorial Period: 1821–1845
American Statehood: 1845

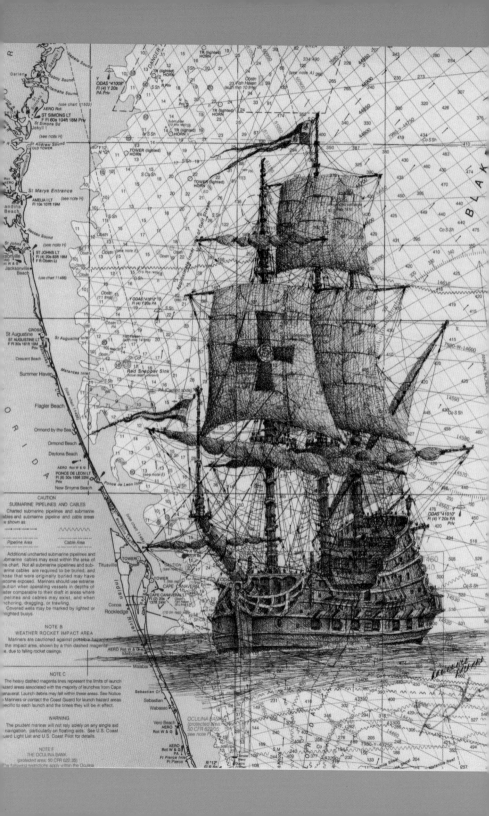

2

The Spanish Landing, 1565

On September 8, 1565, Pedro Menéndez de Avilés splashed ashore in northeast Florida and established San Agustín de la Florida in the name of the Spanish king. As the drama unfolds below, you are there!

The Founding and Thanksgiving

It is September 6. Outside St. Augustine's treacherous sandbar, Menéndez's lead ship, *San Pelayo,* and four smaller ships drop anchor in deep water. On board are eight hundred soldiers, sailors, women, and children from various regions of Spain and Africa.

Captains Andrés López Patiño and Juan de San Vicente with two hundred men disembark in small boats (tenders) and cross the dangerous bar into the inlet, the arm of the sea. They reconnoiter the area for the most convenient place to unload supplies and dig a defensive trench in which to collect the people so they can defend themselves with artillery before a fort can be built.

An enemy attack is imminent. Menéndez had encountered Jean Ribault's French fleet the night before at the mouth of the St. Johns River forty miles to the north. Ribault's ships had come to supply Fort Caroline, built by French Protestants (Huguenots) in 1564 and commanded by René de Laudonnière. Ribault knows where Menéndez is unloading. In 1562 and 1564, he and Laudonnière had sailed by the island (today called Anastasia) and had noted the ocean inlet that now leads into the Spanish encampment.

On September 7 and 8, Menéndez's smaller ships enter the inlet on incoming tides. Soldiers, married men, wives, and children disembark with provisions, artillery, and munitions. Pedro Menéndez disembarks after noon on September 8 in a small boat launched from the *San Pelayo*, which is still anchored off the coast. He crosses the sandbar and lands with ceremony, trumpets, artillery fire, and Catholic ritual led by his chaplain, Francisco López de Mendoza Grajales. Menéndez is sworn in as *adelantado*, captain-general and governor, and officially takes possession of St. Augustine, named after the fifth-century Catholic saint and bishop of Hippo (Algeria).

The day and the saint hold particular significance and symbolism for Pedro Menéndez. September 8 is the feast day of Our Lady of September, the patron saint of Menéndez's home region of Asturias in northern Spain. A solemn mass is held in her honor.

Our Lady of September

Eyewitnesses at the 1565 landing and founding of St. Augustine noted that September 8 was the feast day of Our Lady of September, the Virgin of Covadonga, patroness saint of the Asturias region in northern Spain where Menéndez was born. According to Spanish legend, her appearance gave great hope and courage to a small band of Christians led by a nobleman, Don Pelayo, first king of Asturias, and inspired them to defeat the Moors in A.D. 772. Their victory is the symbolic beginning of the Reconquest of Spain. Huge crowds today continue to pay homage to her shrine in a cave at Covadonga in the Picos Mountains, close to the site of the victory.

Pedro Menéndez de Avilés, 1519–1574

St. Augustine's founder was born to a noble family in the city of Avilés along the rugged coast of northern Spain's Asturias region. He went to sea at a young age and was foremost a sailor, an innovator in ship design and navigation, and a highly respected admiral. He was also an entrepreneur. He set his sights on and devoted his personal wealth to the conquest of the Province of La Florida and future land grants stretching from the Gulf coast and the Florida Keys to the Chesapeake Bay. As Florida's governor and captain-general, he defeated the French and quickly established two towns, St. Augustine and Santa Elena (present-day Port Royal, South Carolina), provisioned his colonies and, in 1573, was summoned by the king to Spain to build an armada and defend the West Indies. He and his wife, Doña María de Solís, had three daughters and one son. Juan, their son, was lost at sea in a hurricane in 1563. Menéndez unexpectedly died on September 17, 1574, in Santander, Spain, at age fifty-five.

❖　❖　❖

Menéndez's Lead Ship, *San Pelayo*

Pedro Menéndez's flagship (*capitana* of the fleet) was a new 906-ton galleon built at his own expense in Vizcaya, Spain, one of the most powerful ships afloat. He named it after Saint Pelayo, a tenth-century boy who chose martyrdom after his capture by the Muslims. The *San Pelayo* arrived in St. Augustine heavy with settlers in 1565, while the timbers of the New England Pilgrims' *Mayflower* were still growing in the ground. Eventually, the *San Pelayo* was captured by English sailors, sailed to Europe, and lost in the North Sea off Denmark.

Observing Indians seem friendly. One eyewitness writes that Menéndez has "the Indians fed and dines himself." Their thanksgiving cocido (stew) undoubtedly has a Spanish shipboard flavor—salt pork, beans, and garlic, hardtack and wine—hopefully enlivened with Indian corn, squash, a fresh fish catch, and berries.

Unbeknownst to the Indians, Menéndez has a contract with his Catholic king to establish two or three Spanish cities as a base for conquest and exploration and for governing the Atlantic coast of La Florida, which was claimed for Spain and named by Ponce de León in 1513 and stretches from the Keys to Newfoundland.

In the dark early hours of September 10, Menéndez sends the partially unloaded *San Pelayo* away to prevent its capture by the French. He writes the king on September 11 that he will inspect the site that seems the most suitable to fortify, because "where we are is not suitable." He plans to do this before the enemy finds them. He writes that he can make the move and build defenses in eight days.

The place where Menéndez disembarks, unloads, and encamps has long been inhabited by Timucua. In 1565, they are subject to a local chief (cacique) called Seloy. The paramount chief of the larger Timucua region that stretches northward and includes the St. Johns River inlet is Saturiwa. It will not be long before Saturiwa wants to be rid of the Spanish.

The Massacres

Ribault and his French fleet arrive at the ocean inlet to St. Augustine, but they do not attack. They sail around looking for the

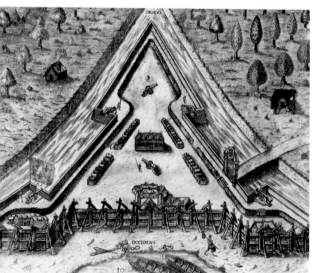

San Pelayo. A strong northeaster starts to blow, and the winds carry the French ships southward to their destruction. For eight days the nor'easter blows, and Menéndez decides to march north in the storm to surprise Fort Caroline, commanded by Laudonnière. He takes

the fort, killing the French defenders but sparing women and children. Laudonnière and the artist Jacques le Moyne escape. Menéndez renames the French fortification Fort San Mateo, assigns Spanish soldiers to defend it, and returns to St. Augustine.

News arrives that French survivors of the storm-destroyed fleet are gathered at an inlet south of St. Augustine. Menéndez marches south and orders the killing of all but a few who are Catholic. When a second group of stragglers arrives at the inlet, they, too, are put to death in the sand dunes, including Jean Ribault. The inlet and the river thereafter are called Matanzas (massacre).

Three years later the French have their revenge. A Frenchman, Dominique de Gourges, sails from France and, allied with Saturiwa, destroys Fort San Mateo and hangs the dead Spanish defenders in the trees. Spain, however, has won Florida. Archaeologists are still looking for the remains of Fort San Mateo and Fort Caroline.

The Move to Anastasia Island

Rid of the French, the Spanish form their St. Augustine government and its headquarters, quickly building their defenses and the first humble houses covered with thatch like those of the Timucua. Archaeologists have found evidence of sixteenth-century Spanish buildings and artifacts buried in the grounds of the Fountain of Youth Archaeological Park north of the Castillo de San Marcos. They are also finding evidence of an Indian village and a mission with Christian Indian burials as well as prehistoric Indian occupations. Centuries of human habitation and nature's changes to the land present many puzzles for archaeologists to solve about the events of the year 1565.

Nine months after the landing, the Spanish are no longer welcome in Timucua territory and are forced to move their settlement to Anastasia Island. Reduced in number by deaths, mutinies, Indian encounters, exploration, and military assignments, the settlers begin anew to build a fortified town near the edge of the island to command the inlet. Reinforcements arrive from Spain in June 1566; the fort and town grow.

Six years later, after their fort and town have been battered by storms, the island's coastal erosion, a mutiny, and a fire, the Spanish colony moves back to the mainland but south of their first encampment. Indian resistance has lessened due to Spanish gifts, pacification measures, and Indian depopulation by European epidemics. Today the remains of the Anastasia Island's fortified town are probably underwater at Salt Run.

Anastasia Island

Many Florida place-names today reflect the names of Catholic saints. Historian Susan Parker's research leads her to believe Santa Anastasia was the name of the patroness saint of an early 1700s chapel at the island's coquina lookout house. (It is not named for the missing grand duchess of Russia!) The British heightened the Spanish lookout; the Americans converted it into a lighthouse. In 1880, eroded by storms, it slipped into the sea and into oblivion except for the name of its patroness saint. A new lighthouse built during 1871–74 soars over the island today, and its stairway offers visitors spectacular views.

1572–1573: A New Town Plan

On the banks of the Matanzas River, protected by Anastasia Island, the settlers in 1572–73 lay out the town we know today. It is barely fourteen years old when Sir Francis Drake, Queen Elizabeth's privateer, raids and burns its wood buildings to the ground. A map drawn in 1586 and published in 1588 depicting the English corsair's triumph is the earliest view of any city in the United States. It shows the sixteenth-century town's streets and houses laid out in a grid aligned with the compass. The parish church stands at harbor's edge; the governor's house is at the top of the Plaza. Thanks partly to Drake's self-promoting map and the charred remains he left behind, archaeologists have found evidence of the sixteenth-century town south of today's Plaza.

Towering over St. Augustine today is a spectacular 208-foot-tall steel cross commemorating the first permanent European foothold in North America. Erected at the Diocese of St. Augustine Mission Nombre de Dios, it overlooks the inlet through which Pedro Menéndez and his followers arrived—their faces mirroring their fears, anxiety, and courage as they step onto an uncharted shore far from their mother country.

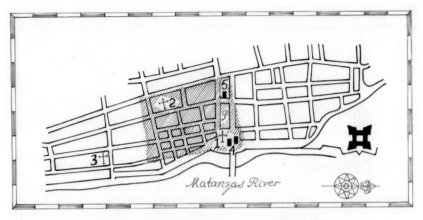

Sixteenth century San Agustín

Spain's Royal Ordinances

St. Augustine's colonists might have followed ordinances issued by King Philip II in 1573 for colonizing and laying out new towns. The king's rules specified that seacoast towns should begin with the main plaza, that the plaza should begin at the landing, and that the church be placed where it could be "seen on leaving the sea" (entering the harbor). Other rules specified that narrow streets should not face into prevailing winds, and that lots should be large enough to sustain kitchen gardens, wells, and animals, and be clean. With narrow streets and house walls built up to the street edge, the whole town served as a defense.

3

Discovering St. Augustine in Ancient Maps

Boazio Map Depicting St. Augustine in 1586 (published 1588)

This drawing is the earliest view of any United States city. It was drawn by Baptista Boazio to illustrate and publish Francis Drake's successful raid on St. Augustine in 1586. Drake's fleet anchors

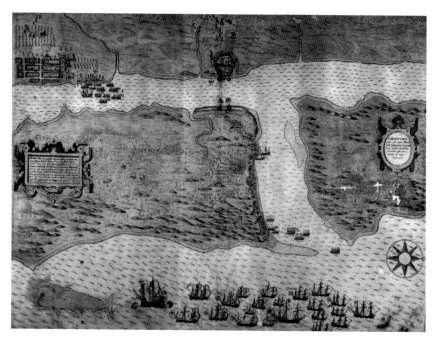

outside the shallow sandbar while small ships' boats enter the inlet and off-load English troops on Anastasia Island. Drake's artillery fires on the fort while his soldiers plunder the city, shown in the upper-left corner of the map. As Drake leaves, he burns all the residences, the church, the governor's house, and the wooden fort San Juan de Pinos. Archaeologists have discovered the 1586 city south of today's Plaza.

Detail of Boazio's Map of 1586 St. Augustine

Boazio's map shows that the 1586 city has eleven urban blocks. These blocks are more or less like today's city blocks south of the Plaza. Drake's troops are landing on the public square at the river's edge. At the western end of the landing place is the governor's house (M) and watchtower (N). At the southeast end near the river's edge is the church (O), a location that was specified in the Spanish king's royal ordinances of 1573. In the cornfield west of the city (upper-left corner), a real-life drama takes place. Captain Anthony Powell, Drake's captain, is killed by local hero Juan Ramírez, illustrated on the map by Powell's riderless horse and the Spaniard's raised sword, which is about to strike the kneeling Powell.

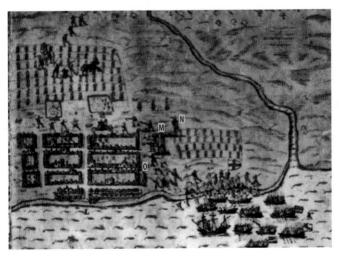

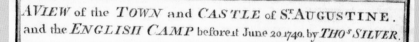
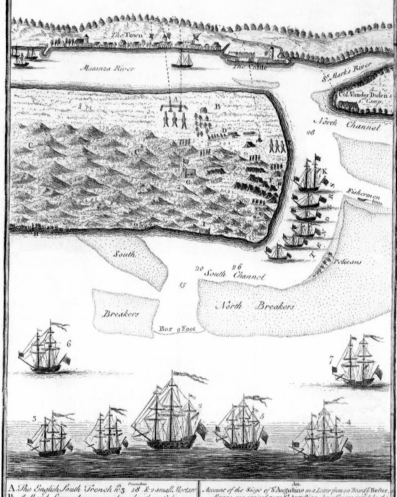

A VIEW of the TOWN and CASTLE of St AUGUSTINE and the ENGLISH CAMP before It June 20, 1740. by THO^s SILVER

This British map documents St. Augustine at the time of General Oglethorpe's attack on the city with 200 seamen, 400 soldiers, and 300 Indians. The shallow inlet forces English ships to stay offshore. Tenders unload troops and supplies while two small mortars in the trench (A) fire on the town and Governor's House (shown with a tower). Sailors drag cannon (D) to fire on the Castillo, which is also fired on from a point of land north of the Castillo. Oglethorpe himself arrives by sea and lands on Anastasia Island's east shore (H). He takes the Spanish coquina lookout (G) and Spanish land battery (I) near the inlet entrance. Wells (L) supply the ships with water. The siege ends July 20 without success, and the defeated English depart.

Elixio de la Puente, *Plano de la real fuerza . . .* 1764 (Map of St. Augustine Buildings)

At the end of the French and Indian War of 1756–63 (or Seven Years' War), Spain ceded Florida to the British. This map is an inventory of buildings within the walled city compiled by the Spanish for the arriving British. A key to the map (not shown here)

identifies all the buildings by owners' names, building materials, and size of lot. Note that the city is still surrounded by the defensive earth barriers called the Rosario and Cubo Lines. The Plaza is at the center; at its west end is the stone Government House; at its east end on the harbor is the consecrated vacant space where the Catholic parish church was burned in 1702. Nuestra Señora de La Soledad (between blocks "b" and "Q") is the new parish church, and the stone convent of the Franciscans is shown at the south end of the city.

A Plan of St. Augustine Town and Its Environs in East Florida from an Actual Survey Made in 1777

Fourteen years after Spain ceded Florida to the British (1763), Joseph Purcell surveyed St. Augustine. His drawing reveals how the British moved into the city. It shows us that the British used the former stone mission church, Nuestra Señora de la Leche

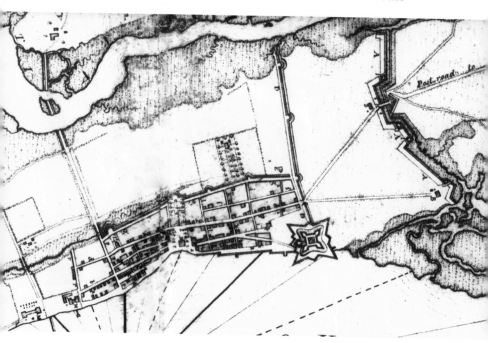

(Our Nursing Mother) north of the Castillo, as a hospital and that they enlarged the Spanish bishop's house on the Plaza to make the British Statehouse (conjecturally pictured below). At the south end of town, they enlarged the Spanish convent of Franciscans as the British barracks, and they built a larger building for additional barracks with a row of kitchens and latrines. On Aviles Street, the Spanish hospital became the British courthouse and jail, and on St. George Street south of the Plaza, the Catholic parish church became the British Anglican church with an added bell tower and spire. The British were planning for a long future in St. Augustine.

4

Time Line

Glance at this time line to see St. Augustine's
Colonial Period history in a nutshell as well as what
was happening at the same time elsewhere.

1500s Timucua occupy
St. Augustine area

1502–1511 Florida peninsula appears on
European maps

1513 Juan Ponce de León lands on
Florida coast

1519 Hernán Cortéz begins conquest of
Mexico

1521 Juan Ponce de León attempts to
colonize Florida

1526 Lucas Vázquez de Ayllón's Florida colony fails

1528 Pánfilo de Narváez marches through Florida

1532 Pizarro conquers Peru and Inca Empire

1539–1540 Hernando de Soto lands near Tampa; winters in Tallahassee

1556–1598 Philip II is king of Spain

1558–1603 Elizabeth I is queen of England

1559–1561 Tristán de Luna's Spanish colony at Pensacola fails

1564 René de Laudonnière builds French Protestant Fort Caroline

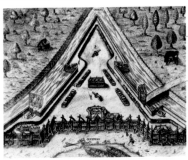

St. Augustine's First Spanish Period, 1565–1763

1565 Pedro Menéndez de Avilés founds St. Augustine, September 8

1565 Menéndez defeats, massacres, and eliminates French from Florida

1566 St. Augustine settlement moves to Anastasia Island

1572–1573 St. Augustine settlement rebuilds on mainland, south of today's Plaza

1574 Menéndez dies in Santander, Spain, September 17

1585 English attempt colony at Roanoke; abandoned 1587

1586 St. Augustine burned by Sir Francis Drake; town rebuilds

1586 Laudonnière's 1564–65 descriptions of the Timucua published

1587 Mission Nombre de Dios established with resident Franciscan friar

1587–1704 Spanish Franciscan missions established in Florida

1588 Map by Baptista Boazio depicting St. Augustine in 1586 published

1588 Spanish Armada destroyed by English fleet

1591 Theodore de Bry publishes first images of Timucua

1594 St. Augustine–born María is baptized; oldest baptismal document in United States

1598 St. Augustine hospital built

1599 St. Augustine's Franciscan convent burns

1607 English settle Jamestown, Virginia

1610 Spanish establish Santa Fe, New Mexico

1620 English establish Plymouth, Massachusetts

1624 Dutch settle New York

1655 English take Jamaica

1668 St. Augustine sacked by English pirates

1670 English settle Charleston, South Carolina

1672–1695 St. Augustine's Castillo de San Marcos constructed with coquina stone

1686 St. Augustine attacked by French pirates

1698 Spanish colony founded at Pensacola

1702 St. Augustine burned by Col. James Moore of Carolina

1704 Cubo Line built to protect St. Augustine's north limits

1713 Two-story coquina stone Governor's House completed

1718 Rosario Line built to protect
St. Augustine's west and south
limits

1728 Mission Nombre de Dios
destroyed in Colonel Palmer's raid

1730 Mission Nombre de Dios stone
church, Nuestra Señora de la Leche
(Our Lady of Milk), rebuilt. Church
destroyed 1793. Shrine dedicated to
Our Lady of Milk (*right*) built 1918.

1732 George Washington born

1733 James Oglethorpe founds
Savannah, Georgia

1738 Fort Mose built, first free black
town in United States

1740 St. Augustine attacked by
Gen. James Oglethorpe; Fort Mose
destroyed

1742 Fort Matanzas constructed at
Matanzas inlet

1746 St. Augustine's Franciscan
missions dissolved by Spanish
Crown

1752–1763 Second Fort Mose built and occupied

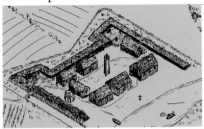

1763 Treaty of Paris, Spain cedes Florida to the British

1763 St. Augustine's Spanish population departs

St. Augustine's British Period, 1763–1783

1763 British divide Florida into East Florida and West Florida; St. Augustine is capital of East Florida

1764 First British governor of East Florida, James Grant, arrives in St. Augustine

1776 Americans declare independence

1777 Minorcans granted asylum in St. Augustine

1783 American Revolution ends; second Treaty of Paris, British retrocede Florida to Spain

It is 1784 by the time the British leave and Spanish arrive

Second Spanish Period, 1783–1821

1789 U.S. Constitution ratified; George
Washington president

1793–1797 Stone Cathedral
constructed

1804–1806 Lewis and Clark expedition
to Pacific Ocean

1808 City Gate rebuilt with coquina

1812 United States declares war on
Britain

1817–1858 Seminole Indian Wars

1821 Florida ceded to United States
(1819 Adams-Onís Treaty, ratified 1821)
and becomes a U.S. Territory

1821 Mexico achieves independence
from Spain

St. Augustine's U.S. Territorial Period, 1821–1845

1821–1836 Spanish Governor's House converted to U.S. courthouse and post office

1824 Tallahassee selected permanent capital of Florida

1825 Castillo de San Marcos re-named Fort Marion

1831 Trinity Episcopal Church built

1837 Osceola captured under white flag; imprisoned in Fort Marion

1845 Statehood; Florida admitted as twenty-seventh state

A Few Additional Dates

1861 Florida secedes from Union and joins Confederate States, January 10

1862–65 St. Augustine is a Union stronghold

1888 Henry Flagler opens his Hotel Ponce de Leon, January 10; new chapter in St. Augustine history and tourism begins

1933 Fort Marion transferred to National Park Service

1942 Fort's Spanish name, Castillo de San Marcos, restored

1964 Martin Luther King Jr. comes to St. Augustine to support civil rights movement

1968 Flagler College established

PART II

❖

❖

❖ St. Augustine,
Street by Street

At the time of the Declaration of Independence in 1776,
St. Augustine was two centuries old. Leave behind the
fast lanes of larger and newer cities: walk into the nation's oldest city and find comfort in its agelessness, its
quaint size, its passion for history. But not everything is
old in the colonial walled town. St. Augustine today is
a young college town that enjoys what youth brings to
the story of the city's longevity.

This guidebook's tours are designed for you to meet
the early settlers and the families who came after
them from many areas of the world to build the city
of centuries. Their restored and reconstructed houses
are described and brought to life with their personal
stories. Learn whose historic house is now a residence
or a trendy tavern, restaurant, or art gallery, a retail store
or bed-and-breakfast inn. You can take carriage, train,
and trolley rides, harbor tours, and nightly ghost walks,
but with the self-guiding walks you can explore on your
own and come upon the unexpected—like an archaeologist unearthing a new discovery or treasure.

All walks in this guidebook start and end at the Plaza,
an easy landmark for getting your bearings. Coffee, ice
cream, drinks, and food are always close by.

Another Shovelful of Earth

Make your tour of the Oldest City an exciting discovery by stopping at archaeological excavations and asking questions of the city archaeologists or SAAA volunteers (St. Augustine Archaeological Association). Members of the SAAA are professional, amateur, and armchair archaeologists trained to assist the city archaeologists in excavations and in the laboratory identifying artifacts and restoring ceramic vessels. Check out

the website at http://saaa.shutterfly.com for news of discoveries at current digs or of monthly presentations and guided field trips.

5

Plaza Walk

Introducing the Plaza

Many have stood on this Plaza before you—barefooted, in hand-made flax clothing, or in monk's robes, Union wools, or Victorian silks. St. Augustinians followed King Philip II's sixteenth-century rules and began their Plaza at the landing central to arriving ships, supplies, and new settlers. It was midway between the fort to the north and the Franciscan monastery to the south. At its west end stood the house of government and at its east end, the *iglesia mayor,* the parish church. Since then the Plaza has been the

center of the colonial city, connecting residents to government and church, harbor and merchants, to city celebrations, religious processions, and military troops on parade. Slaves were sold at its east and west ends. After the Civil War, the Plaza atmosphere was enlivened with orange blossoms, music events, fountains, and strolling visitors viewing alligators on display. Here monuments stand to the local heroes of America's wars and civil rights movement. The nation has declared St. Augustine's Plaza-centered town plan a National Historic Landmark. In the annual November through January "Nights of Lights," its large oak trees are illuminated with thousands of white lights drawing throngs of people to celebrate its magical canopy of stars.

PLAZA WALK MAP

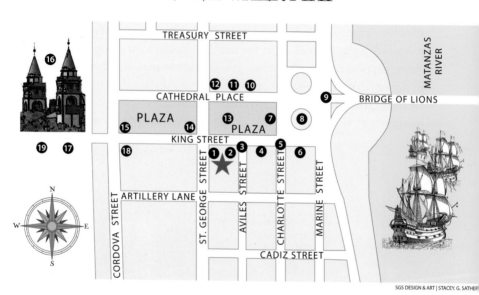

SGS DESIGN & ART | STACEY. G. SATHER

Start your Plaza walk at Trinity Church ★

(1) Trinity Episcopal Church, 1831. Corner King and St. George Streets

Trinity Episcopal Church faces the Plaza opposite the Catholic Cathedral. It is built on the site of the 1735 Spanish Bishop's House and the 1774 British Statehouse, and it might have some of their foundation stones in its walls. It is the oldest Protestant church building in Florida, and the first in the Gothic Revival style. The spire was added by 1843, when the parish could afford it. *Cornelius and the Angel*, a stained glass window by Louis Comfort Tiffany, was added in 1905, and in 1903 the church was expanded to the west with a new entrance facing St. George Street designed by Mark Twain's renowned Connecticut architect, Edward Tuckerman Potter. The 1831 church is preserved as the north transept and Chapel of St. Peter.

Trinity Episcopal Church, St. Augustine, Fla.

(2) **Woolworths Department Store**, 1955. 31 King Street

Woolworths, one of a chain of five-and-dime stores, anchored the Ponce de Leon Shopping Center, the city's first downtown shopping center. It stretched from here to Artillery Lane (a block once owned by Venancio Sánchez) and was designed by Morris Lapidus, acclaimed for his famous Fontainebleau Hotel in Miami Beach (1954). St. Augustine's Woolworths is a landmark in the civil rights movement. Students from Florida Memorial College in St. Augustine held a sit-in at its lunch counter on March 6, 1960, to protest racial discrimination. In July 1963, four African American teenagers sat at the counter and asked for a Coke and hamburger: Joann Ulmer, age 15; Audrey Edwards, age 16; Samuel White, age 14; and Willie Singleton, 16, were arrested and spent six months in jail and reform school until released by order of the governor and cabinet in January 1964. Woolworths is gone, but not forgotten in civil rights history. Its lunch counter is preserved and can be viewed in the Woolworths space.

(3) **Entrance to Aviles Street**, the oldest street in the United States, in continuous use since the sixteenth century (see South of the Plaza, Tour A)

(4) Florida State Center/Heritage House, 1964. 6–11 King Street

The State of Florida constructed this building to showcase Florida history during the city's four-hundredth anniversary celebration. Its architecture represents that of the U.S. Territorial Period wooden City Hotel and grocery that was owned by the Connecticut merchant Seth Wakeman. During the Heritage House construction, centuries-old burials were unearthed. It had been the site of the sixteenth- to seventeenth-century parish church, Nuestra Señora de los Remedios, and its cemetery, which were close to the riverbank before the seawall extended the land eastward. Remedios was burned by Francis Drake in 1586 and rebuilt. There, in the light of a glowing candle, the infant María was baptized in 1594. The rebuilt church was burned by the English in 1702. Its consecrated lot was marked by a cross and remained vacant until the U.S. Territorial Period, Seth Wakeman's building, and several later hotels.

María's Baptismal Record, 1594

María, infant daughter of Juan Jiménez and María Melendez, was baptized June 10, 1594, in the sixteenth-century parish church that was built on the riverbank in St. Augustine. Her baptismal record, signed by candlelight by Father Diego de Sanbrana, is the oldest in the United States. When the Spanish left Florida in 1763, they took the church records of births, baptisms, marriages, and deaths with them to Cuba. They were discovered in Havana in 1871, damaged by bugs and mold, and were brought back to the United States in 1906, where they are conserved in the Historical Archives of the Diocese of St. Augustine.

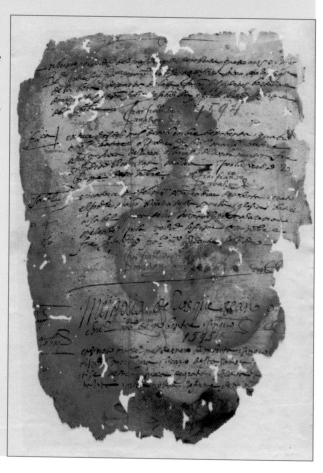

(5) Entrance to Charlotte Street, one of St. Augustine's narrow, sixteenth-century colonial streets (see South of the Plaza, Tour B)

(6) Plaza Building (A1A Ale Works), 1888. 1–5 King Street

The Plaza Building began as John Wesley Estes's "Supreme Department Store," or "Surprise Store." Later it was the Gilbert Hotel, then Hamblen's Hardware Store. Potter's Wax Museum took the second floor in 1949; the Plaza Hotel was on the first floor (1950s–1960s). Today's grand staircase is from Henry Ball's 1870 mansion on Valencia Street (later the Barcelona Hotel, razed 1962). Long a brewery and restaurant, the verandas overlook the harbor and catch the ocean breezes. This site might have been the sixteenth- and seventeenth-century Nuestra Señora de los Remedios cemetery; in early local myth, burials were exposed in storm surges before the seawall was built.

(7) Public Market/Slave Market, 1824. East End of Plaza

On April 12, 1887, sparks from the burning St. Augustine Hotel and the Cathedral across the street ignited the public market roof. Later repaired, the 190-year-old market approximates the Hall of the Market Place and Meat Market described in British eighteenth-century documents as having a cupola and bell. Two market buildings depicted in early-nineteenth-century images might reflect an earlier Spanish tradition: in 1598, Governor Méndez de Canzo established meat and fish markets with weights and measures on the Plaza. After the Civil War, the one remaining building was labeled "slave market" on postcards. From the sixteenth century until 1865, many slaves were privately and publicly traded, sold, and bought by city residents and government and church officials. Deed Books (1820s–1840s) record public sales of slaves in the market and in the courthouse yard. In the 1960s, the old market building was a rallying place for the civil rights movement.

(8) Statue of Juan Ponce de León, 1923

East of the Public Market, a boat basin enabled people to dock at the Plaza. In 1895 it was filled in, and on the site today stands a bronze statue of Don Juan Ponce de León high on a pedestal. Ponce de León was not the first European to see Florida, but he is credited with its 1513 Spanish name, "La Florida." His first landing place is unknown, and his search for a fountain of youth is a seventeenth-century myth, but note that his arm points north to St. Augustine's Fountain of Youth Park. He died in 1521, at age forty-one, from a Calusa arrow wound inflicted near Tampa. The statue was the gift of Dr. Andrew Anderson and was cast from a mold of the 1881 original, which was cast in Puerto Rico from British cannons and stands in San Jose Plaza near the explorer's grave in the Cathedral of San Juan.

(9) Bridge of Lions, 1927

The South's most handsome span, the Bridge of Lions, is noted for its graceful arches and tile-roofed towers framing the bascule (drawbridge) opening. It spans the Matanzas River and creates a grand entrance to and from St. Augustine's Plaza. Gracing its west end is a pair of sculpted lions given to the city by Dr. Andrew Anderson. Carved in Italy of white Carrara Tuscany marble, the lions are copies of those that guard the entrance to the Loggia dei Lanzi (1382) in the Piazza della Signoria in Florence. Each bridge guardian weighs more than five thousand pounds. After the bridge was declared endangered in 1997 by the National Trust, residents fought for its authentic restoration; the four-year project was completed in 2010. Before it was built, the way to Anastasia Island, the lighthouse, and the beaches was by ferry or horse-drawn cart on wood boards and rails, and in 1915 by an electric trolley. Listed in the National Register of Historic Places.

(10) **Bank Building**, 1928. 24–28 Cathedral Place

There were no height restrictions in St. Augustine when this 133-foot-tall skyscraper was constructed. Its height, scale, and proportions compared to the city's historic skyline and colonial Cathedral next door prompted the city to enact height limits. Until 2013, banks were the building's main tenants. Some of the building's eye-catching elements are the Mediterranean-style terra-cotta embellishments.

(11) **St. Augustine Cathedral**, 1797; **Renwick Belltower**, 1888.
36 Cathedral Place

Mariano de la Rocque, chief engineer of the Second Spanish Period, drafted the new parish church plans in 1789–93. He left Florida in 1793, and the engineer Pedro Díaz Berrio supervised its construction through its completion in 1797, enlarging the classical entrance and belfry façade. Residents donated materials and labor, and coquina blocks were recycled from earlier mission churches. Its bells were hung in niches and were rung by mallets from a wood platform. In 1887, flames from a fire in the

hotel next door destroyed the church roof and interior, but the shell-stone walls and Doric entrance stood firm. James Renwick Jr., the architect of St. Patrick's Cathedral in New York City, restored the century-old church building. He also designed its new "chimes"— the beautiful neoclassical bell tower standing today—financed by Henry Flagler and constructed with the poured-coquina-concrete method used at Flagler's hotels. In 1965, the Cathedral was enlarged; the interior and altar were greatly changed; the coffered ceiling was raised; and the exposed truss beams were painted. Miami Cubans made the hydraulic floor tiles that replaced wood floors. The baptismal font is a replica of the original one in Santeverás de Campos, where Juan Ponce de León was baptized in 1474 (now in the Cathedral of San Juan, Puerto Rico, where he is buried). St. Augustine Cathedral was designated a National Historic Landmark in 1972 and a Minor Basilica in 1976, symbolized above the entrance in white marble by the crossed keys of St. Peter and the triple-crowned pope's tiara. The east courtyard is dedicated to Father Félix Varela.

Father Félix Varela, 1788–1853

In the Cathedral's small east courtyard is a likeness of Father Varela. He was born in Havana and spent his childhood in St. Augustine, where his grandfather was an officer at the Castillo. Ordained at age twenty-three in Cuba, he became an early advocate of human civil rights, freedom for slaves, and Cuban independence from Spain. His opposition to the Spanish monarchy led to his 1823 exile in New York, where as vicar general he served the city's poorest, particularly Irish immigrants. When he became ill, he moved to St. Augustine; he died in 1853 in the small wood schoolhouse on the east side of the Cathedral. He was buried in the Varela Chapel at Tolomato Cemetery, but his remains were transferred to Havana in 1911. Cuban bishops have opened his sainthood cause (1980s) and await his beatification and, ultimately, canonization.

❖ ❖ ❖

James Renwick Jr., 1818–1895

For a half century, the celebrity American architect, James Renwick, designed many of America's most famous and beautiful buildings, including the Smithsonian's Romanesque Castle in Washington, D.C., the Gothic St. Patrick's Cathedral in New York City, and other noted churches, theaters, hotels, schools, and country houses across America. Renwick owned property and a winter house in St. Augustine. When the Cathedral's roof and interior burned in 1887, he offered to plan its restoration. His elegant neoclassical campanile graces today's Plaza.

(12) Minorcan Courtyard, Cathedral West Courtyard, 1975

In the Cathedral's west courtyard, a statue and monument are dedicated to the Minorcans and Father Pedro Camps, their beloved spiritual leader. Father Camps, born in Mercadel, Minorca, accompanied the Minorcans to the Turnbull Plantation in New Smyrna, Florida, in 1768 and to St. Augustine in 1777. In that year, the Reverend John Forbes's elegant stone home with six classical columns stood here; he was minister of the British St. Peter's Anglican Church on St. George Street (see **8** in South of the Plaza, Tour A). Father Camps died in 1790, and his remains were moved into the Cathedral after it was completed in 1797.

The Minorcans

"Minorcan" is a term locally used for the 1,403 Minorcans, Greeks, and Italians who came to New Smyrna, Florida, in 1768 to work as indentured laborers on Andrew Turnbull's indigo plantation. Their St. Augustine story begins when Francisco Pellicer, Antonio Llambias, and Juan Genopoly secretly walked and swam seventy-five miles to St. Augustine in 1777 to complain to British governor Patrick Tonyn about the suffering, deaths, and overextended servitudes at Turnbull's plantation. Governor Tonyn terminated their indenture contracts and granted them asylum. About six hundred penniless Minorcans walked to St. Augustine and settled in the area north of the Plaza known as the Minorcan Quarter or Little San Felipe. They supported their families by fishing, farming, and various trades, soon becoming prosperous citizens engaged in shipping and mercantile industries.

(13) Spanish Constitution Monument, 1813

A white stone obelisk bears a plaque dedicated to Spain's 1812 constitution. Notice of the constitution was sent from Spain to all its colonies with instructions to install celebratory tablets and rename all plazas, Plaza de la Constitución. St. Augustine constructed an obelisk for the tablet using stones from the old Bishop's House and British Statehouse, but Spain's constitution was short-lived, and when the monarchy returned in 1814, it ordered the removal of all celebratory tablets and plaza names. St. Augustine removed the plaque—then reinstalled it in 1818, when Spain again had a constitutional government. Listed in the National Register of Historic Places.

(14) Government House.* 48 King Street

Since the sixteenth century, a building important to Spanish, British, and American governments stood at the Plaza's west end. After the
first wood buildings, the two-story Governor's
House was built with stone in 1713 and was
portrayed in a British painting in 1764. A mansion by colonial stan-
dards, it had a classical entrance, a tall stone watchtower, a walled
courtyard and garden, a stable and coach house, and an elaborate
east-facing balcony that has been reconstructed. Today's building
reflects the many Spanish, British, and American architectural traditions, changes, and uses and the various restorations and reconstruc-
tions: from a governor's residence and capitol to a U.S. courthouse
planned by Robert Mills (designer of the Washington Monument), to
a 1930s post office. Its eighteenth-century stones echo the stories of
the people who governed or were governed: people who climbed its
watchtower; slipped out its secret door; were sold as slaves in its yard;
sought promises of refuge and freedom; signed important documents;
or indulged in lavish entertainment. One resident Spanish governor
suffered the anguish of a father whose daughter eloped. John and
William Bartram and the American Revolutionary War hero Maj. Gen.
Nathanael Greene ate in its dining room. Greene described his elaborate dinner hosted by the Spanish governor, Vicente Manuel de Zéspedes, in 1784 as having 150 tasty dishes served up in seven courses.
Walk inside to discover Government House's restored elegance and
changing exhibits. Listed in the National Register of Historic Places.

Grant's Wicked Bottle

During his first year in office (1764), Governor James Grant and his guests drank 236 gallons of rum, 140 gallons of Madeira, 76 gallons of tenereff, 1,200 bottles of claret, 519 bottles of Port, and similar amounts of Champagne, sweet wine, porter, and beer. His food list was equally bounteous. His chefs were three enslaved black men trained in French cooking. "Pickled and gouty," according to historian Michael Gannon, Grant's health may have hastened his return to England in 1771.

❖ ❖ ❖

Governor Zéspedes's Daughter Elopes

Governor Zéspedes's daughter Dominga, described as having sweet, languishing eyes, eloped in 1784 with Lt. Juan O'Donovan, an Irishman serving the Spanish Crown in the Hibernia Infantry Regiment. His proposal of marriage was rejected by Governor Zéspedes because the lieutenant was not of noble birth. In a clever ruse, Dominga sneaked away from a festive party in the Governor's House and met her lover in the home of Doña Angela Huet, English wife of the Spanish chief engineer, Mariano de la Rocque, who was absent that evening. A servant was sent to fetch Father Miguel O'Reilly to attend to Angela, who feigned sickness. As the priest walked in the door, he heard the young couple loudly reciting their marriage vows, which hearing constituted a marriage, no matter how clandestine. Deeply upset, Zéspedes arranged a proper marriage that same night in order to save Dominga's honor; he then arrested her husband and sent him to Havana for two years. They were later reunited in St. Augustine and lived happily together.

(15) Flagler Fountain

Behind Government House in the Plaza's west
garden, there is a large fountain donated by Henry
Morrison Flagler, the cofounder of Standard Oil,
the founder of the East Coast Railway, and the
entrepreneur developer-builder of Florida's east
coast palatial hotels. Soaring over the fountain
and in view of the Plaza are the terra-cotta roof
tiles and spires, towers and crenellated pediments
of his Spanish Renaissance–style hotels. When
Flagler opened the Hotel Ponce de Leon, Hotel

Alcazar, and Hotel Cordova in the late 1880s, he changed St. Augustine's cultural image and economic future. Step outside the former
colonial walled town and walk into the Gilded Age with visits to these
magnificent buildings vibrant with twenty-first century activities.

Flagler's **Hotel Ponce de Leon (16)**, 74 King Street, is beauti-
fully restored and is the centerpiece of Flagler College and a National

Historic Landmark. Flagler's former **Hotel Alcazar (17)**, 75 King Street, is now City Hall and Lightner Museum; and Flagler's Moorish Revival–style **Hotel Cordova (18)**, 95 Cordova Street, is today's elegant Casa Monica Hotel. Their walls were built with layers of poured-coquina concrete, pioneered by Frederick W. Smith in 1883

S. A. 77—Villa Zorayda, St. Augustine, Florida

at Villa Zorayda, his Moorish-style house that is now **Villa Zorayda Museum (19)**, 83 King Street. These must-see national treasures hold astonishing surprises. At Flagler College, see the largest number of Tiffany windows in any one building; at the Lightner Museum is a dazzling collection of Victorian-period arts, and at the former Hotel Alcazar, you can dine and shop for antiques in what is thought to be the first and largest indoor swimming pool. In the garden fronting the Casa Monica Hotel and the Lightner Museum entrance is a bronze likeness of Pedro Menéndez de Avilés that was given to St. Augustine by the City of Avilés, Spain, where Pedro Menéndez was born and is buried.

6

South of the Plaza Tours

Two self-guided tours take you south of the Plaza into the city's earliest neighborhoods. Tour A and Tour B show you where the Spanish colonists rebuilt their town after leaving Anastasia Island in 1572. They laid down their streets and houses in a gridiron pattern close to the river. It was a good town plan, sensitive to the geography, climate, and prevailing winds. You will be walking in its sixteenth-century pathways because after the British set the wooden town on fire in 1586 and 1702, it was rebuilt to the sixteenth-century plan—the plan that exists today. As you explore the city's oldest area, you are encouraged to respect the privacy of today's homeowners.

SOUTH OF THE PLAZA MAP - TOUR A

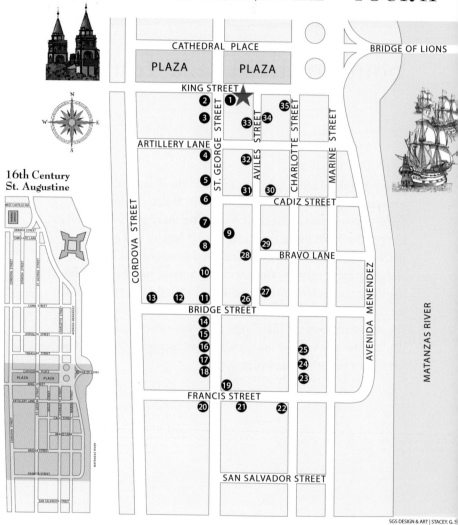

CATHEDRAL PLACE

BRIDGE OF LIONS

PLAZA   PLAZA

KING STREET

16th Century
St. Augustine

ARTILLERY LANE

CORDOVA STREET

ST. GEORGE STREET

AVILES STREET

CHARLOTTE STREET

MARINE STREET

CADIZ STREET

BRAVO LANE

AVENIDA MENENDEZ

MATANZAS RIVER

BRIDGE STREET

FRANCIS STREET

SAN SALVADOR STREET

SGS DESIGN & ART | STACEY. G. 5

SOUTH OF THE PLAZA, TOUR A

Begin Tour A at Trinity Church ★
near the southwest corner of the Plaza

(1) Trinity Episcopal Church, 1831. Corner St. George and King Streets

Trinity's entrance in 1831 faced the Plaza, but in 1903 the little Gothic Revival pointed–style church was expanded and reoriented to this handsome new entrance on St. George Street. Edward Tuckerman Potter, the designer, also designed Mark Twain's elaborate Gothic Revival mansion in Hartford, Connecticut. Old Trinity, however, still exists (see Plaza Walk) preserved in the north transept and St. Peter's Chapel, named after the British Period St. Peter's Anglican Church that stood farther south on St. George Street (see **8**). Trinity's expansion stands partly on the site of the colonial Spanish Bishop's House (1735) and British Statehouse (1774), and the 1880s St. George Hotel.

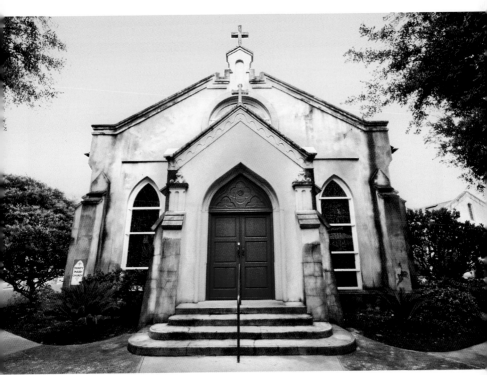

(2) Lyon Building, 1886–1887. Corner St. George and King Streets

Two stone houses in 1763 faced the Bishop's House (where Trinity Church stands), one owned by Lorenzo Rodríguez, the other by Don Diego de León. Seventy years later, Major Benjamin A. Putnam's large wood house had replaced them. Putnam (1801–1869) fought in the Second Seminole War (1836) as commander of the Mosquito Raiders and was an attorney, judge, city mayor, and Florida legislator. Because he was a slaveholder and an officer in the Confederate militia, his house in Union-held St. Augustine was confiscated and sold. It became a boardinghouse and Walter Lyon's grocery, hardware, and furniture store. Lyon's heirs replaced it with this commercial retail and office building facing a tree-lined King Street in 1887. It was built with the innovative poured-in-place coquina concrete material of Frederick W. Smith's Casa Monica Hotel under construction next door. After Henry Flagler bought Smith's hotel, completed its Moorish architecture, and renamed it Hotel Cordova, the Lyon Building was updated by adding a fourth story and a Moorish crenellated (castellated) tower compatible with Flagler's hotel.

(3) **Horruytiner-Lindsley House**, First Spanish Period. 214 St. George Street

Horruytiner family history in St. Augustine begins with Louis de Horruytiner, governor of Florida from 1633 to 1638. His nephew, Sergeant Major Pedro Benedit Horruytiner, of Zaragoza, Spain, accompanied him to Florida and was acting governor in 1648 and 1651, and royal accountant in 1674. Benedit Horruytiner's high standing is revealed in an inventory of his private library and estate, a wood house near the harbor, slaves, and cultivated fields north of town. His son, Captain Lorenzo Horruytiner, might have begun the current stone house shortly after the 1702 fire; in 1763, it was owned by Don Diego Horruytiner y Pueyo. Bought by Horace Lindsley in 1896, his son, Mayor James E. Lindsley, sold it after the brutal 1974 murder of his wife, Athalia Ponsell, a former model and political activist, on the front steps of the house at 124 Marine Street. Her murder remains unsolved. Recently renovated, it is listed in the National Register of Historic Places.

(4) Paredes-Seguí-Macmillan House, First Spanish Period. 224 St. George Street

Don Juan de Paredes, sacristan of the parish church, Nuestra Señora de la Soledad (see **8**), owned the coquina first story of the current house in 1763. After the British Period, with its tile roof in disrepair, the house reverted to the Spanish Crown and was occupied by Juan Aguilar of the Canary Islands. His granddaughter married Bernardo José Luis Seguí, son of the Minorcan Bernardo Seguí who built the Seguí–Kirby Smith House **(32)**. Bernardo José Luis Seguí in 1823 added the wood second story that is present today. The house remained in the Seguí family until 1882, when it was bought by the Ammidowns of Massachusetts and rented to Col. Andrew T. Macmillan, whose family lived here for forty years before buying it in 1925. In 1964, its owners restored its 1823 form.

(5) Palm Row, 1904–1906. 230 St. George Street

Holmes Phillip Ammidown, a wealthy Massachusetts merchant, bought this land in 1882 near his own large winter house that stood until 1955 (now a parking lot). After he died, his son, Henry Phillip, developed the land as an English-style mews lined along a private brick walkway landscaped with palms trees. Palm Row stayed in the Ammidown family until 1941, when the houses were sold to individual owners. Spanish coins were found by Palm Row workers in 1905, and later archaeologists found a sixteenth-century well and pottery fragments. Don Francisco Ponce de León's masonry house had occupied the area in 1763.

(6) Stanbury Cottage, ca. 1857–1869. 232 St. George Street

This house is a splendid example of the picturesque American Gothic Cottage. The style was popularized in Andrew Jackson Downing's books (1840s–1850s) and inspired by Alexander Jackson Davis's cottage designs. The Stanbury builder is unknown, but it might have been Bartolo Masters (Maestre), who owned the lot from 1854 to 1867, or Francis Triay, who bought the lot in 1867 for one thousand dollars and sold part of it with the pleasant cottage residence for two thousand dollars in 1869 to W. S. Pendleton of New York. Four years later, J. Downing Stanbury, an attorney, bought the house—his widow stayed in the house and lived to be one hundred years old. She entertained Mrs. Henry Flagler and the artist Martin Johnson Heade in the cottage said to be always bright with roses and fragrant jessamine. Today's longtime owners, Robert W. Harper III, and his

wife, Alicia Harper, are preserving its many intricate details: the ornate Carpenter Gothic gable bargeboard and diamond-shaped multipaned windows that prompted its local nickname, the gingerbread house. Listed in the National Register of Historic Places.

(7) **Villa Flora**, 1898. 234 St. George Street

Reverend and Mrs. O. A. Weenolsen of Minneapolis, Minnesota, built their yellow brick house as an elegant winter residence. The Romanesque and Moorish elements may have been inspired by Frederick Smith's Villa Zorayda (see **19** in Plaza Walk), but the raised coquina basement is an unusual feature in St. Augustine. Villa Flora was known in its time for its stained glass and leaded windows, flower gardens and palms, and the walkway lighted with gas lamps from St. George to Cordova Street and called Flora Promenade. Three cottages built along the promenade were rented out for the winter season. In 1906, Villa Flora was the residence of Alanson Wood, whose widow, Bessie Wood, ran it as a small hotel until the 1920s, and by 1934 it was the restaurant Villa Flora Grill. The Sisters of St. Joseph acquired the house in 1940 and have used it as a school and now a residence.

(8) La Soledad/St Peter's (site), First Spanish and British Periods. 236 St. George Street

Under this grass parking lot are some of the oldest burials in St. Augustine—and remains of the sixteenth-century Spanish hermitage, shrine, and hospital, in which the sick could see the altar. A Crown-owned slave woman, María Joije, served the hospital of Santa Barbara. The shrine was dedicated to Nuestra Señora de la Soledad (Our Lady of Solitude) and del Santo Christo and was one of the few structures to survive the 1702 English siege. It became the city's parish church and was enlarged with stone in 1735, when a coquina belfry façade with three arches and three bells was added. The British in 1764 converted it to St. Peter's Anglican Church, reversing the altar to the east and adding an entrance tower and tall steeple at the west end. The acting governor, John Moultrie, called it an ornament to the young colony. Dismantled in 1793, its stones are recycled in the walls of today's Cathedral. La Soledad's site is owned and conserved by the Sisters of St. Joseph.

(9) Motherhouse of the Sisters of St. Joseph, 1874. 241 St. George Street

Prominent Spanish residents Don Juan José Solana (parish priest), Don Felipe Benedit Horruytiner, Joaquin Alvertos de Florencia, Don Antonio Nieto, and Francisco Xavier Dias owned the houses along this block in 1763. A century later, with the arrival of the Sisters of St. Joseph, construction of the current building began. The Sisters were brought to St. Augustine in 1866 from Le Puy-en-Velay by Bishop Augustin Verot, France, to establish charities and schools for white and black children. In the century and a half since the convent began, the Motherhouse has been changed and enlarged. Lourdes Hall at the corner of Bridge Street is the Sisters' retirement home. The block to the south is the Cathedral Parish School.

(10) William Dean Howells House, 1910. 246 St. George Street

This four-bedroom 1910 frame house was rented in 1916 to William Dean Howells (1837–1920), the novelist and editor considered to be the dean of American letters. His closest friend was Mark Twain.

Howells invited to tea the young Sinclair Lewis, who was then launching his writing career. As the future Nobel Prize winner began to tell Howells about the wonderful reviews of his first book, Howells is known to have interrupted sweetly to tell him that he would later forget those kind words and remember only the critics that who roast him unmercifully.

(11) Huertos-Canova House/Prince Murat House, Second Spanish Period. 250 St. George Street, corner of Bridge Street

Antonio Huertos's coquina house has stood at this street edge since 1815. The house and adjacent land was bought by Antonio Canova in 1821 and held until his death in 1869—his family had come from Corsica a century earlier to work on Dr. Andrew Turnbull's New Smyrna plantation and had joined the Minorcans who found refuge in British St. Augustine in 1777. Ralph Waldo Emerson, renowned American writer, visited St. Augustine for two months in 1827 and is thought to have stayed at Canova's boardinghouse. Amos Spear added the whimsical 1880s Victorian-period balcony with jigsawn balusters and novelty shingles. Greta Garbo, the silent film star, dined here when it was a restaurant in 1939, but its most colorful occupant was Prince Achille Murat, Napoleon's nephew.

Prince Achille Murat Legend

Crown prince of Naples, Charles Louis Napoleon Achille Murat, 1801–47, nephew of Napoleon Bonaparte, emperor of France (1804–14), fled France after Napoleon's exile and settled in Florida. In local St. Augustine legend, the colorful Murat stayed in the Huertos-Canova House in 1824, lowered himself fully clothed in a chair in the Matanzas River to keep cool, and dined on turkey buzzard, boiled owl, alligators, and snakes. In Tallahassee in 1827, he met and married Catherine Daingerfield Willis Gray, great-grandniece of George Washington, and they traveled the world before he died in 1847. In 1854, his widow bought and lived on the 520-acre Bellevue Plantation (now part of the Tallahassee Museum). Until her death in 1867, she was active in saving Mount Vernon, George Washington's home.

(12) Canova-Dow House, 1840, 42 Bridge Street; (13) Canova–de Medicis House, 1841, 46 Bridge Street

Detour right (west) on Bridge Street to see two rare U.S. Territorial Period houses. When Antonio Canova bought the Huertos-Canova (Murat) House in 1821, he also bought the adjacent land, and on it he built a small weather-boarded house for his son Paul. It was later moved to 42 Bridge Street and today is the two-dormer house behind a coquina wall. Canova had built a second small house for his eldest son, John, that was later conveyed to Ramon Canova and held in trust for John's children when John was lost at sea. Later owners, Amos Spear (in 1886) and Emanuel E. de Medicis (in 1899), operated it as a boardinghouse. Both houses were acquired by Kenneth Dow for the Dow Museum of Historic Houses.

(14) Bronson Cottage, 1876. 252 St. George Street, corner Bridge Street

The Bronson Cottage was designed as a wedding present for Robert and Isabel Donaldson Bronson of Barrytown, New York. Alexander Jackson Davis, the architect, designed houses for Robert's and Isabel's parents in New York when Davis was one of America's foremost designers, known for his Gothic and Italianate cottages and many Hudson River mansions. Robert's parents, Dr. Oliver and Joanna Donaldson Bronson, were winter residents in St. Augustine. Isabel, the bride, whose budget for the home was five thousand dollars, wrote that she wanted a "simple inexpensive Cottage of wood . . . two storied . . . raised above the ground 2½ to 3 feet which is advisable in this climate . . . with a garret above merely for current of air and a veranda above the lower one on the east side as is so agreeable in a southern house." Davis called it an Etruscan veranda. Other Italianate features included bracketed eaves and a low hip roof. The two chimneys still had terra-cotta pots in 1918, and on the lot were a windmill, a fountain, and a detached kitchen with servants' quarters.

(15) De Medicis–Graftstrom House, 1851–1853. 256 St. George Street

Remodeled and moved back on the lot, this 1850s house was turned into the De Medicis Boardinghouse early in the 1900s by its owner, Mary Barnes. She named it after a relative, Emanuel de Medicis, the 1890 owner whose family descended from Italian members of the Minorcan colony that came to St. Augustine in 1777. Ruth Sigrid Grafstrom, an American artist, lived here after a career as an illustrator for fashion design and commercial products. She designed for Saks Fifth Avenue, Coty perfumes, Bergdorf, and MatsonLine Cruise Ships; her artwork appeared in *McCalls* and on the covers of *Cosmopolitan*, *Woman's Home Companion*, and *Vogue* (1930s–1940s).

(16) Renwick's Cast Concrete Wall, 1888. 262 St. George Street

James Renwick Jr., architect of St. Patrick's Cathedral in New York and the St. Augustine Cathedral's bell tower, designed a graceful stone wall in 1888 to enclose the Cathedral property. It was demolished during Cathedral renovations in 1965, but this remnant was rescued. In the 1820s, the coquina Presbyterian Church was built here on what was then a larger lot. A wooden chapel with a bell tower was added in 1870 but was moved to the west end of the Government House lot in 1877, pulled there with ropes and pulleys by Plains Indians imprisoned at Fort Marion. When the Flagler Memorial Presbyterian Church was built, the old Presbyterian church was demolished and the lot was divided into the three current properties: on the west lot today stands the brick synagogue built (1923) by the First Congregation of B'nai Israel that faces Cordova Street; the north and south lots now hold the wood frame houses at 262 and 264 St. George Street that were built between 1910 and 1930.

(17) **Upham Cottage**, 1893. 268 St. George Street

More than a century and a half after Juana Esquivel's tabby house stood here, Col. John Jaques Upham (1837–1898) of the Eighth Cavalry retired to St. Augustine and built his house. He was a West Point graduate (1859) and a veteran of the Civil War battles at Malvern Hill and Gettysburg, and of the Sioux War and the Big Horn and Yellowstone Expedition of 1876. His colorful 1892 octagonal Victorian Queen Anne–style house is decorated with eclectic details and originally had a large ballroom, a conservatory, and a roof garden.

(18) Hibbard Cottage/Magnolia Inn, 1888. 272 St. George Street

Curtis A. Hibbard, a legislator from Burlington, Vermont, and former lieutenant in the Vermont Ninth Infantry, bought this property from his friend and fellow Vermont native Amos Spear. Hibbard sold it to Mollie Pease, also of Burlington, a Spear relative who turned it into the Hibbard Cottage Apartments. Several owners later, it was the Magnolia Inn operated by Martin Firestone. Changes have occurred to the original tower and porch, but the Victorian-Flagler era details are preserved. The 1966 owner returned it to a private residence.

(19) García-Dummett House/St. Francis Inn, Second Spanish Period. 279 St. George Street, corner St. Francis Street

Gaspar García built the first two stories of this coquina house in 1791. Rafael Savedra de Espinosa was the owner in 1795, and Col. Thomas Henry Dummett in 1835. Dummett, an officer in the British marines, came to Florida from Barbados and built a steam-powered sugar mill and rum distillery in 1820. The family fled to St. Augustine in the Second Seminole War, and Dummett Plantation was burned (the ruins are in Ormond Beach). He died in 1839, and his daughters Anna and Sara turned the house into a boardinghouse. John L. Wilson added the third floor and Mansard Second Empire–style roof popular in St. Augustine in the 1880s. Renovated and improved over the years, the St. Francis Inn is one of the oldest inns in continuous use in the United States. Its current parking lot was once the site of the three-

story wood Valencia Hotel built by James Alexander McGuire, Henry Flagler's hotel contractor, where in 1905, President Theodore Roosevelt dined on a seafood dinner—he was staying at the Hotel Ponce de Leon, sleeping in Henry Flagler's bed.

(20) **Stickney House**, 1873. 282 St. George Street, corner St. Francis Street

Bernardo Nieto's stone house stood here when St. George Street was a footpath. A century later, the current large Mediterranean masonry house was built for Judge John B. Stickney. Later it became the Keewatin Boarding School for boys, and later still, during 1916–21, it was temporarily used as Flagler Hospital after Alicia Hospital (built by Henry Flagler) burned. It was remodeled as a residence by the architect Fred A. Henderich after he designed the new 1921 Flagler Hospital.

> Optional Tour: Continue south on St. George Street to see 1905–1920s St. Augustine–style bungalows that are distinctive for their cabbage palm–trunk porch columns, natural cypress shingles, and coquina fireplaces. Fred A. Henderich, the architect, graduated from Columbia University and went to work with Flagler's East Coast Hotel Company, but he left the company to build these houses.
>
> ❖ ❖ ❖
>
> Resume Tour A from **García-Dummett House** (St. Francis Inn) east on St. Francis Street toward the river.

(21) **Fernández-Llambias House**, First Spanish Period. 31 St. Francis Street

Pedro Fernández owned this coquina house in 1763, when it had only one story, a flat roof, and window openings protected by Spanish-style wood *rejas* and shutters. Today's house owes its look to the British Period additions and a 1950s restoration/reconstruction—notably the second story, street balcony, pitched roof, and south-facing arcaded loggia and

porch under which is the outside staircase. There were good and bad times, auctions and foreclosures, and a succession of owners: Juan Andreu, native of Minorca; Dr. William Hayne Simmons, a planter and one of two commissioners who selected Tallahassee as Florida's capital; José Manucy, a cigar maker; and Catalina Usina Llambias, who acquired it in 1854 and whose family owned it until 1919. The house was jointly bought in 1938 by the Carnegie Institution of Washington and the St. Augustine Historical Society. Restored

in the 1950s, it is held in trust for the City of St. Augustine. This was one of St. Augustine's earliest house restorations based on extensive research. It has been designated a National Historic Landmark and is listed in the National Register of Historic Places.

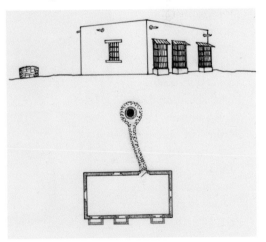

Catalina's Secret Burial

Catalina Usina Llambias wanted to be buried in Tolomato Cemetery with her relatives. She died in 1886, shortly after the cemetery was closed and burials were forbidden. Her son Joseph secretly arranged for a gravesite to be opened. He was fined fifty dollars, but to this day his mother rests in peace in the Tolomato Cemetery.

(22) Checchi House, 1885–1893. 25 St. Francis Street, corner Charlotte Street

Named for its longtime owners after 1940, Dr. John Checchi and his wife, Stella, this Queen Anne–style house has been extensively renovated by the Florida National Guard and used since 1980 for offices.

Turn left (north) onto Charlotte Street. At the corner of St. Francis and Charlotte Streets is the Colonial-period Tovar House, which is described in Tour B as part of the Oldest House complex on St. Francis Street.

(23) Alexander-O'Donovan-O'Reilly House (Headquarters of the St. Augustine Historical Society, founded 1883), 1964. 271 Charlotte Street

William Alexander was granted the property by the British Crown in 1778. He was a member of the Indian trading firm of Panton, Leslie and Company. Later owners of Alexander's house include Juan O'Donovan, the lieutenant in the Hibernia Regiment who eloped with Governor Zéspedes's daughter in 1784; Father Miguel O'Reilly in 1789; and Antonio Alvarez in 1814 (see **González-Alvarez House/Oldest House [23]** in South of the Plaza, Tour B). Reconstructed by the Historical Society, it is entered through the side garden wall and the door protected in the arcaded loggia under the second-story porch. Today's garden wall encloses the Society-owned Tovar House and Oldest House museum complex, with its many exhibits and a gift shop.

(24) Alexander-Garrido House, 1966. 267 Charlotte Street

William Alexander's colonial outbuilding was the model for this one-story house reconstructed at the street's edge by the St. Augustine Historical Society. The house name also reflects the owner of record from 1838 to 1865, Manuel Garrido. Its style—with flat roof, rainspouts, window grilles, and side entrance—is typical of small Spanish-built St. Augustine houses. Window sashes with glass panes came into favor during the 1770s British occupation.

(25) Manuel de Herrera House, 1955. 257 Charlotte Street

Most of the earliest original coquina houses along Charlotte Street had disappeared by the 1890s. This sixty-year-old reconstruction by the St. Augustine Historical Society is one of the earliest attempts in the city to accurately portray a colonial period St. Augustine–style house.

Turn left (west) on Bridge Street, then right (north) on Aviles Street.

(26) Gaspar Papy (Papi) House, also known as Whitney's Oldest House and Don Toledo House, Second Spanish Period. 36 Aviles Street

Gaspar Papy was born in 1750 in Smyrna, Greece, and arrived in St. Augustine with the Minorcans in 1777. Papy prospered with a general store, a farm north of the city gate near the stone church, Nuestra Señora de la Leche, and a ferry across the San Sebastian River. He built two attached coquina houses ca. 1803–17 to replace his first wood house. One of the attached houses was torn down, and Papy's son sold the remaining house in 1836 to Angelina Williams, a free woman of color (see **Rovira-Hernández House [15]**, South of the Plaza, Tour B). In 1903, it was acquired by Everett C. Whitney, grandson of Eli Whitney, inventor of the cotton gin. Whitney also owned the Ponce de Leon Fountain of Youth attraction and the St. Augustine Alligator Farm, and he promoted his new acquisition as "Whitney's Oldest House Built in 1516" (a half century before St. Augustine was founded). Not shy about his tourist tactics, he planned to have a huge tank in the yard with a swimmer of reputation riding on the back of an alligator. In 1924, Frederick Hewitt, an antique dealer, added the front balcony and touted it as the house built in 1516 by Don Toledo, a Spanish conquistador, for his Indian bride. By that time the house was dilapidated enough to play the role. In 1928, it was bought and rehabilitated by the Sisters of St. Joseph.

(27) Fontane House, ca. 1835. 33 Aviles Street

Joseph Fontane owned this house an unknown number of years before he died in 1835; his son John was the owner of record in 1849. Successive occupants included African American tenants, an upholsterer and mattress maker, and the Ben Bow Tavern. It was altered for apartments and stuccoed in 1950. Renovated by the current owner for a single residence, the stucco was removed and old pre-1835 wood siding was exposed.

(28) Father Miguel O'Reilly House, First Spanish Period. 32 Aviles Street

Father O'Reilly's House is one of the oldest houses in the city. Some of its current walls might include portions of the pre-1702-siege tabby and rubble walls. A stone house on this lot was recorded in 1763, owned by Don Lorenzo Joseph de León, a cavalry ensign and scout to Fort San Diego in 1739 and a *guarda mayor* (keeper of provisions and munitions) in 1752. After the British Period, Father O'Reilly bought the house for his rectory. He had recently completed his studies at the sixteenth-century Irish College in Salamanca, Spain, and came to St. Augustine to be chaplain for the troops. He was assistant parish priest during the Cathedral planning and construction (1788–97) and served as its first pastor and as vicar of East Florida (1797–1812). He lived in the house until his death in 1812 and willed it to the church community. After the Civil War, eight Sisters of St. Joseph arrived (1866) from Le Puy, France, and opened St. Cecelia School for black children in Father O'Reilly's House. Restored by the Sisters to its 1840s appearance and rehabilitated in 2002, the historic O'Reilly House and garden are open to the public. Listed in the National Register of Historic Places.

The Hurricane Lady

Father Miguel O'Reilly's House Museum holds a statue of great mystery called *The Hurricane Lady*. The story goes that during a storm around 1800, a Spanish vessel heading to St. Augustine nearly sank off the coast. Throwing items off the ship to lighten it, the crew found a Virgin Mary statue in the hold. The captain held up the statue, and he and the crew prayed for deliverance from the storm, promising that if they were saved, the statue would be placed in the home of a religious family. It went to various Minorcan houses, where shrines were created with much veneration and repair of her clothing and hair. Some believe she might be Saint Barbara. Or could she be Our Lady of the Conception made in Barcelona for the new 1797 Cathedral? Her ship was captured by French pirates, and her crate ended up in Charleston, then Cadiz, and Havana before her trail to St. Augustine runs cold.

(29) Ancient Well, Cofradia del Santissimo Sacramento, First Spanish Period. 29 Aviles Street

The Cofradia (Brotherhood) of the Most Holy Sacrament owned tabby houses here in 1763. The Cofradia was a religious organization of soldiers and residents founded early in the 1600s. A well on the property discovered by archaeologists was lined with coquina blocks. It might date to about 1690, when Governor Diego de Quiroga released stones from the royal coquina quarry to people who could pay for them—but only after the quarry master, Juan Colens, had assured the governor in that year that there was enough coquina

to complete the fort. Juan was John Collins, an English farmer from Barbados who intended to settle in Charleston but was captured in 1670 in Santa Catalina by the Spanish and brought to St. Augustine. He decided to stay in St. Augustine, where he rose in the ranks and married a local girl. When the well was excavated in 1990, archaeologists found charred remains of furniture and kitchen utensils, perhaps from the British-set fire of 1702.

(30) Don Manuel Solana House (Casa De Solana Inn), Second Spanish Period. 21 Aviles Street (original entrance, 220 Charlotte Street)

Twenty-three-year-old Manuel Solana (1740–1821) stayed behind in St. Augustine when the Spanish left in 1763 in order to sell Spanish boats, houses, and horses to the arriving British. His family's roots in St. Augustine dated to the early 1600s. One of his relatives in 1763 was Don Juan José Solana, the parish priest, who had houses on Charlotte and St. George Streets. Manuel would profit by the regime change. He married Mary Mitchell of London, England, and stayed through the British Period and Second Spanish Period and became a wealthy cattle rancher. He married María Maestre (Masters), a Minorcan, in 1781 and owned several houses, including this coquina house built between 1808 and 1820. It stayed in the Solana family until bought in 1867 by Dr. Oliver Bronson, a wealthy New York physician and prominent St. Augustine winter resident. Charles F. Hamblen, a Maine native, owned it in 1883 as well as two Hamblen Hardware warehouses next door on Aviles Street that are leased to

retailers to-
day. Hamblen
also owned
"Blenmore," a
large Victo-
rian house on
the bayfront.
Solana House
has been
remodeled by
a succession
of owners
who enclosed
the loggia,
added the
Aviles Street
balcony, the
annex, and
the courtyard.

(31) Ximénez-Fatio House, Second Spanish Period. 20 Aviles Street, corner Cadiz Street

Andrés Ximénez, a merchant from Ronda, Spain, and Juana Pellicer, his Minorcan wife, built this two-story house with Spanish and British elements as their residence and store in 1797. Juana's father, Francisco Pellicer, had led the Minorcans to St. Augustine in 1777. Flush with the street with thick coquina walls, a side entrance, and a cantilevered street balcony, it has exterior stairs leading to the second floor. Juana and Andrés chose glazed windows, a chimney and fireplace for heat, and tabby and wood floors, and they built a detached masonry kitchen on the foundations of an earlier structure. They raised five children here before their early deaths. A succession of women after 1823 owned and operated the complex as a boardinghouse. Louisa Fatio (*above left*) made it one of the city's most fashionable inns during 1851 to 1875. Her heirs sold it to the National Society of the Colonial Dames of America in the State of Florida in 1939 with a deed restricting architectural changes. It is restored and open to the public as an authentic house of the 1790s–1880s. Archaeologists in 2002 unearthed in the yard's 1650s trash pit a rare Caravaca Cross, (*above right*) symbol of the True Cross brought by friars to the New World and thought to protect the city. Listed in the National Register of Historic Places.

(32) Seguí–Kirby Smith House (St. Augustine Historical Society Research Library), Second Spanish Period. 12 Aviles Street, corner Artillery Lane

This early 1800s house has a remarkable history. Bernardo and Agueda Villalonga Seguí bought the lot in 1786 with a house of stone and wood and a detached kitchen listed in 1763 in the name of Don Antonio Urbana de Melo. His wife, Doña Manuela Menéndez Marquez, however, had inherited it in 1743 from the estate of her father, Don Francisco Menéndez Marquez, whose large house was next door (see **33**). Seguí built the current coquina house in 1805, incorporating a part of the earlier building. The Seguí family had arrived in St. Augustine with the Minorcans in 1777, where Bernardo became a baker and supplied Spanish troops with bread. As a member of a merchant network with many sailing vessels and as a captain in the militia, he amassed considerable capital, along with many properties and slaves. In this house he fathered thirteen children. The second-floor porch (now enclosed) overlooked the garden and the freestanding kitchen bakery where he made bread. A balcony over Aviles Street was removed in the late 1800s, but the arcaded loggia is an original and rare survival. When Florida became a U.S. territory (1821), Superior Court Judge Joseph Lee Smith of Connecticut rented the house. His widow, Frances, was forced to leave the city and her house was confiscated because of her Confederate activities.

Her son, Gen. Edmund Kirby Smith (1824–1893), surrendered the last Confederate force almost two months after Gen. Robert E. Lee surrendered at Appomattox. The *Daily Press*, the *St. Augustine Evening Record,* and the Free Public Library occupied the house before it became the Society's Research Library. A bronze sculpture in the garden, *Sons of St. Augustine*, depicts Dr. Alexander Darnes and

Gen. Edmund Kirby Smith, both born in the house, one the African American physician and the other a Confederate general who became a professor at the University of the South in Sewanee, Tennessee.

(33) Aviles Street, 1570s, and Ponce de Leon Shopping Center, 1955

Aviles Street was long called Hospital Street; its name was changed to Aviles Street in 1924. A treasury official, Don Francisco Menéndez Marquez, had owned a large two-story house on the street's west side that was converted when he died in 1743 to the Spanish Military Hospital. The British turned the hospital into their courthouse and jail in 1770; it was destroyed by fire in 1818. The

entire block between Artillery Lane and the Plaza was acquired by Venancio Sánchez, a member of one of the city's oldest and most wealthy Spanish families. The Sánchez Block in 1955 became the city's first downtown shopping center, the Ponce de Leon Shopping Center with Woolworths its anchor store (see **2** in Plaza Walk). Restaurants and shops occupy the historic shopping center today. Aviles Street is popular with tourists who like to explore.

Francisco Menéndez, Black Militia Leader

Francisco Menéndez, the Mandinga commander of the Fort Mose militia, may have arrived in St. Augustine as a fugitive from Carolina in 1725. He was sold in 1729 to Don Francisco Menéndez Marquez, the treasury official whose name he took. He joined the black militia and led other slaves as their de facto captain in raids against former English owners and in petitioning the Spanish governor and bishop for their freedom, which was granted by Governor Montiano in 1738, the year they built Fort Mose. After bravely fighting in the Battle of Bloody Mose in 1740, Francisco petitioned the Spanish king for his official captain rank and salary as a reward for his services. His request was refused, and he became a corsair to earn money to petition the king of Spain. Captured by the British, he was flogged and sold into slavery. He returned to St. Augustine in 1759, having either escaped or been ransomed, and again served at Fort Mose, which had been rebuilt in 1752. Francisco and his wife and family evacuated to Cuba with the Spanish in a ship named *Our Lady of Sorrows*.

(34) **Spanish Military Hospital,*** 1966. 3 Aviles Street

William Watson, a British carpenter, remodeled a long wood stable for his residence on the east side of Hospital (Aviles) Street in the 1760s (then across from the British courthouse and former Spanish hospital). In 1779, Watson moved and converted his former stable-residence to a convalescent house. After the Spanish returned to St. Augustine (1784), they converted Watson's building to a new military hospital. It had separate rooms for officers and soldiers, an apothecary shop, guard room, doctor's procedure room, kitchen, and morgue, and an apartment on the second floor. Hot water was heated in the fireplace. After extensive archaeological investigation, the Second Spanish Period hospital was reconstructed with masonry and is open to the public to demonstrate colonial medical practices.

(35) **William Watson House,*** 1968. 206 Charlotte Street

Behind (east of) his first residence (now the Spanish Military Hospital), William Watson built his second city residence. Watson was the English carpenter hired at the New Smyrna plantation of Andrew Turnbull in 1767 to build Turnbull's residence, plantation stores, indigo-processing buildings, four bridges, a wind mill, and 145 houses for Minorcan laborers. He was also an active carpenter-builder in St. Augustine who purchased and renovated old buildings. No ordinary carpenter, he had twenty slaves cutting timbers and roof shingles and had in his possession books of architecture. Following his departure for England in 1784, Watson's vacant house was given to Father Pedro Camps; after Camps died in 1790, the house was given to his ward, Martín Mateo Hernández. It is thought to have burned in 1887. The house has been reconstructed using British carpentry techniques.

End your tour at the Plaza.

SOUTH OF THE PLAZA MAP - TOUR B

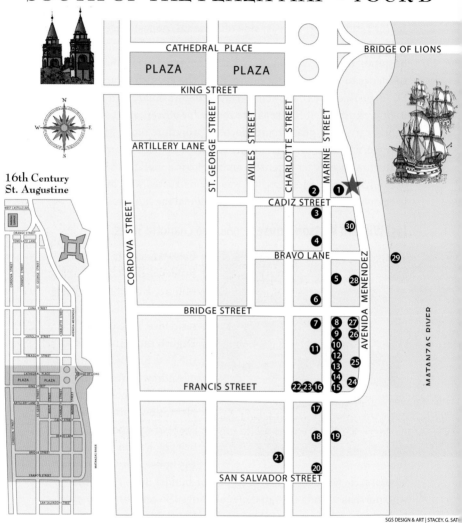

16th Century
St. Augustine

CATHEDRAL PLACE

PLAZA   PLAZA

BRIDGE OF LIONS

KING STREET

ARTILLERY LANE

ST. GEORGE STREET

AVILES STREET

CHARLOTTE STREET

MARINE STREET

CORDOVA STREET

CADIZ STREET

BRAVO LANE

BRIDGE STREET

FRANCIS STREET

SAN SALVADOR STREET

AVENIDA MENENDEZ

MATANZAS RIVER

❷ ❶ ★

SOUTH OF THE PLAZA, TOUR B

Start Tour B at the Worth House ★ across from the City Marina.

(1) **Worth House**, 1961. 118 Avenida Menendez

The original Worth House stood for 170 years on the west side of Marine Street facing the river. It was dismantled in 1961 and reconstructed across the street to its early 1800s appearance using some of the original coquina. William Livingston and his daughter Hester had resided in the original house, running it as the Union Hotel from 1815 to the 1830s. The house was named for its owners from 1869 to 1904: Margaret Stafford Worth, widow of Gen. William J. Worth; her unmarried daughter, also named Margaret; and her older daughter Mary Worth Sprague, wife of Capt. John T. Sprague. William Worth, then a colonel, had arrived in St. Augustine in 1840 as commander of all forces in Florida, and he successfully brought the Second Seminole War to an end in 1842. Later, during the Mexican War under Gen. Winfield Scott, Gen. Worth was the hero in the capture of Monterrey and Vera Cruz (1846–47). Lake Worth, Florida, and Fort Worth, Texas, are named after him.

(2) Elixio de la Puente House Site

A large, prestigious colonial-period coquina house stood in this parking lot early in the 1700s. It was sold and resold to important officials
with the changes in governments. Don Juan Joseph Elixio de la
Puente, the Spanish treasury official, owned it until 1764. It was sold
to William Drayton, the incoming chief justice of British East Florida
in 1765 and a member of the wealthy Drayton family of Charleston,
South Carolina. When he left, Frederick William Hecht, deputy
commissary general of New York, Boston, and Charleston, bought
the house, and he sold it to Miguel Lorenzo Ysnardy, captain of the
frigate *Santa Anna,* and the Cathedral's building contractor (1793–97).
It was a U-shaped house around an inner courtyard in which there
was a coquina well shaped like a scallop shell, symbolic of St. James,
patron saint of Spain and the Knights of Santiago. The house was in
ruins by 1855, and was no longer standing after the Civil War.

(3) St. Augustine Art Association, 1954/1998. 22 Marine Street, corner Cadiz Street

A group of artists and
writers met in 1924
at the Ximénez-Fatio
House on Aviles Street
(See [**31**], South of
the Plaza, Tour A)
and formed the Gal-
leon Club, now the
Art Association. This
Mediterranean Revival
fine arts gallery was
built in 1952 for its
permanent collection

and monthly exhibits. When new wings were added in 1998, Carl
Halbirt, the city archaeologist, made an exciting discovery. In a pit
six feet deep he found hundreds of pieces of charred ceramics and
burnt wood, the large-scale remnants of Francis Drake's raid in 1586
that left the wood city in ashes. Reconstructed ceramic vessels are
permanently exhibited in the North Gallery above the excavated site.

(4) Victorian Frame House, 1894–1899. 30 Marine Street, corner Bravo Lane

This is the first of several notable Victorian-period houses along this street. In contrast to colonial St. Augustine's white stuccoed geometric houses, this late Victorian-period example is colorfully embellished with paint, tiered porches, carpenter's jigsawn spindle work, and Stick-style finials added to the gable.

(5) Rodríguez "Mystery House," First Spanish Period. 35 Marine Street

What looks today like a blank wall is a centuries-old house that was often owned by free black women. Its unexpected story lies inside the **Bayfront Inn** (see **28**).

(6) Kenwood Inn, 1886. 38 Marine Street, corner Bridge Street

The Kenwood has been a bed-and-breakfast inn for more than a century. In 1894, the large Victorian-period frame structure was advertised as "Miss LaBorde's Boarding House" with delightful water views. In 1910, it was sold to Margaret Morgan and became the Kenwood. The façade's two-tier verandas with jigsaw elements and the third-floor balustraded gable dormer are popular features of late-nineteenth-century southern architecture, but they are unique in this ancient city more known for its colonial Spanish and British architecture.

(7) Countess De Montjoye House, 1889. 11 Bridge Street, corner Marine Street

A Queen Anne tower and spacious porch dominate this Victorian-period wood house built by S. Bang Mance in 1889 for Grace L. Hickock of Cairo, Egypt, who was married to a Bavarian count. The house is one of a few surviving late-nineteenth-century Victorian period houses in St. Augustine.

(8) Long-Sánchez House, Second Spanish Period. 43 Marine Street (a.k.a. 7 Bridge Street)

George Long in 1804 bought Francisca Rosy Dulcet's wood house (built in 1788 by her father, Josef Rosy) and took it down to build the current coquina house. It was purchased in 1835 by José Simeon Sánchez (1797–1853) (*right*), son of Francisco Xavier Sánchez and Mary Hill. Francisco Xavier Sánchez was St. Augustine's wealthiest cattle rancher (see North of the Plaza Tour). His son José Simeon inherited land, cash, houses, and slaves from his father's and mother's estates and distinguished himself as a member of Florida's first constitutional convention in 1838. The Sánchez family, through its marriages with members of the Pérez, Solana, and Espinosa families, is one of the oldest in the United States. José Simeon Sánchez's wife, Mary Lopez, was the daughter of Mary Mitchell and Manuel Solana, the young infantry officer who, like Francisco Xavier Sánchez, had stayed behind in the city when the British arrived, acquired land, and prospered (see **Solana House [30]** in South of the Plaza, Tour A). José Simeon Sánchez married again—to a Marin daughter who lived next door **(9)**. The

colonial St. Augustine–style house stayed in the Sánchez family until purchased in the 1930s by Beulah and William Aquilla Lewis, who restored and occupied it during the next thirty years.

(9) Marin House, Second Spanish Period. 47 Marine Street

Francisco Marin built this two-story coquina house in the 1790s
to replace Don Pablos Villa's 1788 wood house. Marin was born in
1770 to indentured Minorcan laborers at the New Smyrna Plantation of Andrew Turnbull. He was seven years old when he and his
parents joined the Minorcan colony fleeing to St. Augustine in 1777.
His father bought the lot, and with the help of a slave, young Marin
built this house for his marriage to Antonia Pons. Their daughter
became the second wife of José Simeon Sánchez (1847) in the house
next door **(8)**. Marin's house originally faced Marine Street, and his
lot sloped to the river, but after the seawall was constructed and the
Civil War ended, the property east of the house was high, dry, and
valuable. Two winter cottages with waterfront views were built on
the former Marin land and later were attached to the older colonial
house by Capt. Henry Belknap, a yachtsman from Shelter Island,
New York. The historic Marin complex today includes the Villas de
Marin (apartments) entered from Marine Street, and the Bayfront
Marin House, a bed-and-breakfast inn facing Avenida Menendez
with wraparound verandas overlooking the harbor (see **27**).

(10) Puello House, Second Spanish Period. 53 Marine Street

A small colonial coquina house constructed during 1812–14 for María Manuela Puello is preserved within this current house. José Simeon Sánchez (see **8**) was among the succession of owners after 1821. After the Civil War, protected by the seawall, the colonial Puello House was enlarged and reoriented to the bayfront at 158 Avenida Menendez (the former Bay Street). Around

the time of World War I, it was more extensively remodeled by J. Clifford R. Foster, son of Mary Delores Sánchez and grandson of José Simeon Sánchez. Foster was a major general in the Florida militia, and as adjutant general of Florida he arranged for the National Guard to be headquartered in St. Augustine at the St. Francis Barracks (see **17**).

(11) González-Jones House, First Spanish Period. 56 Marine Street

Juan Ignacio González in 1763 owned the house of stone on this site; in the British Period (1763–84), John Fairland was the owner. In the Second Spanish Period, one owner was Francisco Xavier Sánchez, the cattle rancher father of José Simeon Sánchez, who himself (or his children and grandchildren) owned at various times three houses on Marine Street to the north. You will meet the wealthy and powerful Francisco Xavier Sánchez when you tour North of the Plaza. In the century after 1904, three generations of the Harry Jones family occupied this house. Enlarged before the Civil War and again in the 1980s, care was taken to retain the original first-story coquina walls. Modernizing additions include some wood siding, a second-story balcony, dormer, and entrance sidelights and transom.

(12) Gibbs-Mickler House, 1830s. 59 Marine Street

Kingsley B. Gibbs built this U.S. Territorial Period house that was later owned and occupied by Henry Mickler. It became a boarding-house in 1839 and apartments after the 1930s, with a shingled extension built toward the river.

(13) **Monson-Pinkham House**, 1840–1854. 67 Marine Street

Behind a stone wall with an ornamental iron gate is a frame U.S. Territorial Period house raised off the ground on coquina piers and heated by a coquina chimney. The 1840 owner was the cabinet maker William Monson (originally spelled Osmunson), born in St. Augustine in 1815 of Norwegian descent. Family member Fritchieff (Fritchie) Monson (1849–1904) operated the San Sebastian River ferry (1865–67), and Anthony Vincent (Bossy) Monson was the proprietor of the late-nineteenth-century wooden Monson Hotel overlooking the river north of the Plaza (now the site of Hilton Historic Bayfront). William Slade Macy Pinkham purchased the Marine Street Monson house at the end of the nineteenth century and extended it toward the waterfront. Pinkham in 1884 also owned **Pinkham's Wharf** (see **29**) and the Ocean View Hotel (site of the **Bayfront Inn (28)**.

(14) **Rovira-Dewhurst House**, Second Spanish Period. 71 Marine Street

Recently painted pink and renovated with French doors and curvilinear balcony supports, this house has a colonial history. Francisco Rovira, a real estate investor, built the first story with coquina flush with the street in 1799 and sold it the same year to Antonia Perdomo, wife of Fernando de la Maza Arredonda, a wealthy merchant and Florida landowner. Four years later, she sold it to Charles Gobert, a New York merchant. Thomas Law owned it from 1825 until 1833, and James Riz from 1833 to 1860. Riz was the operator of the stagecoach from Picolata to St. Augustine. A later owner, Judge Long, purchased the one-story house and rented it to Henry Glover, a black boatman (a boat basin was just south of the house). When William W. Dewhurst, former city mayor and postmaster, owned the house (1902–48), photographs show he added the wood second story, extended the house eastward with a second-story porch overlooking the river, and turned it into a winter cottage rental entered at 170 Avenida Menendez.

(15) Rovira-Hernández House, Second Spanish Period. 73 Marine Street

José Antonio Coruna, a farmer from the Canary Islands, built his wood house here in 1794, but six years later the real estate developer Francisco Rovira replaced it with a one-story coquina and tabby-floor house that he sold in 1803 to James William Lee. It was still a one-story house with a detached kitchen when Lee sold it in 1820 to José Mariano Hernández, who bought it for Sampson Williams, a young free black man and a member of the Hernández household. He was the son of Angelina, a slave woman, and the white planter William Williams (d. 1807), the brother of the deceased first husband (Samuel Williams) of Hernández's wife, Anna Marie Hill. During the Flagler era, William S. Hall, a Chicago attorney, added the second story and an extension toward the river in 1888–94 with a large porch entered at 172 Avenida Menendez. William W. Dewhurst purchased it and used it as a winter rental from 1902 to 1948. The original Rovira-built colonial house is preserved in the northwest section of the house facing Marine Street.

José Mariano Hernández (Gen. Joseph Marion Hernández)

José Mariano Hernández, born on May 26, 1788, and raised in the city's Minorcan Quarter (Little San Felipe), was the oldest of ten children of Martín Hernández Triay, a carpenter, and Dorotea Gomila, daughter of a fisherman. Sent to Cuba to read law, he returned, married Anna Marie Hill of St. Augustine in 1814, and bought a large house on Charlotte Street. Anna Hill was the wealthy widow of Henry Samuel Williams and owner of a 3,200-acre plantation (now Daytona Beach). She raised ten children, fifteen counting four by her deceased husband and a biracial nephew, Sampson Williams. Hernández in 1818 purchased the 800-acre Mala Compra cotton plantation and 375 acres of John Moultrie's Bella Vista on the Matanzas River south of St. Augustine. Mala Compra became the family residence-headquarters for twelve plantations. His name anglicized, Joseph Marion Hernández was appointed Florida's Territorial Delegate to the U.S. Congress (1822), named presiding officer of

the Territorial House of Representatives, and commissioned a brigadier general (1823–24). Mala Compra was burned in the Second Seminole War, and Hernández's seven plantations were in foreclosure by 1851. The general moved to Cuba and died in 1857. Mala Compra's ruins are open to the public. Hernández is known as the man who captured the Seminole leader Osceola under a white flag in 1837.

(16) De la Rosa Houses, 1963 and 1971. 74 and 76 Marine Street, corner St. Francis Street

Two masonry houses constructed in the colonial St. Augustine style by the St. Augustine Historical Society are named for Doña Petrona Perez de la Rosa, the owner of the lot and its stone house in 1763. She was born in the city in 1707, the daughter of a Canary Islander, and she married Corp. Diego Rodrígues Jacinto. When the Spanish returned in 1784, her house was briefly rented by Juan José (Joseph) Bousquet, surgeon at the Royal Hospital. By 1899, the lot was vacant.

(17) St. Francis Barracks/Florida National Guard Headquarters. 84 Marine Street, corner St. Francis Street

A Franciscan monastery of logs, planks, and thatch was built on this site in the late sixteenth century. Friars entered through the wood door of this Convento de la Concepción Inmaculada and received their assignments to Indian villages in the Florida

wilderness. Locally known as the Convento de San Francisco, its church, friary, cloister, and refractory were rebuilt with coquina after it was burned by the British in 1702. Its cemetery now lies under the parking lot. After the Spanish left the city in 1763, the church and friary were converted in the British Period to the St. Francis Barracks with a wharf, boat basin, bakery, and garden plots. Spanish troops in the Second Spanish Period occupied these buildings and Union troops in the 1860s. Rebuilt after a fire in 1915 using some of the earlier coquina and conveyed to the State of Florida in 1921, the St. Francis Barracks today is the Florida National Guard Headquarters.

It owes its symmetrical architecture and wraparound verandas to the British design. In the former friary section, the public can visit remnants of the Spanish-built coquina arcade and Franciscan cells—inquire at the St. Francis Barracks.

(18) Officers Quarters, St. Francis Barracks Post, 1883–1885.
86–98 Marine Street

Officers' quarters at the St. Francis Barracks
army post may have been built at the request of
Gen. Frederick Tracy Dent, who assumed command of the post in 1875. His sister, Julia Dent
Grant (*right*), was the wife of the president
of the United States, Gen. Ulysses S. Grant

(1869–77) (*left*). Dent
and Grant were West
Point graduates who
served together under
Gen. Winfield Scott in
Mexico. Grant met Julia

during a visit at the Dent plantation, White
Haven, in Missouri, and proposed several
times over the objections of both of their
fathers—his because the Dents were slave-
holders; hers because of his army career. In
1880, President and Mrs. Grant, Union Civil
War general and Mrs. Philip Sheridan, and
the Dents visited St. Augustine.

(19) King's Bakery, British Period. 97 Marine Street

The British built this bakery and flour magazine in 1769–71 as part of the St. Francis Barracks. Its coquina walls are two feet thick; at one time there was a large fireplace on the north wall. After the British vacated the bakery, two men lived in the building: David Taylor, a native of Scotland and a baker; and Andrew Devitt, a native of Ireland and a glass window maker. The bakery was separated from the barracks when Marine Street was cut through during the Second Spanish Period. It served as a military hospital after 1821, and in 1934 it was remodeled as a garage for the Florida National Guard.

(20) National Cemetery, 1828/1881. 104 Marine Street

Designated a National Cemetery in 1881, this hallowed land had served as a burial ground since the 1828 interment of Lt. Jackman Davis. In 1842, the burial ground received the remains of the officers and soldiers that were gathered from the battlefields of the Second Seminole Indian War. They were brought to St. Augustine in seven wagons escorted by Col. William J. Worth (see **Worth House [1]**). Among the dead were all the soldiers ambushed in Bushnell under the command of Brevet Maj. Francis Langhorne Dade in 1833 during the Second Seminole War. They were reinterred under the three coquina pyramids. In 2002, the city archaeologist, Carl Halbirt, found a tombstone fragment that marked the graves of nine-month-old Sebree and two-year-old Janet, children of Lt. Sebree Smith, stationed at the St. Francis post in the 1880s; their early deaths from measles and diarrhea reveal how little was understood about disease and sanitation. Before the American burials, this land held the largest building in British Florida, a three-story veranda-wrapped brick-and-wood building called "Pile of Barracks." Even earlier, the land was used by Indians from the nearby mission village Nuestra Señora de la Punta.

Turn right (west) on San Salvador Street then right (north) on Charlotte Street.

(21) Vernacular Wood House, post–Civil War. 320 Charlotte Street

After the Civil War, the area along the west side of the burial ground was a black residential neighborhood. This house is a remaining example of the local vernacular-style frame houses with porches that stood in the area.

Cross to the north side of St. Francis Street (former Convent Lane) and walk east toward river.

(22) Tovar House/Cannonball House, First Spanish Period. 22 St. Francis Street

Built early in the 1700s, this house was owned by Joseph Tovar when the Spanish were documenting properties in 1763 and preparing to turn them over to the British after signing the Treaty of Paris. John Johnson became the new owner, but not for long. Florida was retroceded to Spain by the second Treaty of Paris in 1783, and the house reverted to the Spanish Crown. Juan Coruna and his family, recent arrivals from the Canary Islands, occupied the house until it was auctioned in 1791 to Gerónimo Alvarez with the house next door (**Oldest House**). Alvarez willed the Tovar House to the heirs of his only daughter, Theresa Llambias, who

predeceased him, and it stayed in the Llambias family until after the Civil War. It was rented in 1885 to Gen. Martin D. Hardin, a former aide to Robert E. Lee. After a cannonball was found lodged in the east wall, the house was locally called the Cannonball House. It is owned and restored by the St. Augustine Historical Society.

Gen. Martin D. Hardin (1837-1923)

Abraham Lincoln met his wife, Mary Todd, in the house where Martin D. Hardin was born in Illinois. John J. Hardin, Martin's father, was a close friend of Lincoln. Martin graduated from West Point (1859) and was an aide to Col. Robert E. Lee at Harpers Ferry, Virginia, during the capture of the antislavery activist John Brown. Wounded twice at the Battle of Bull Run, he lost his left arm at Catlett's Station. He recovered and assumed command of a regiment at Gettysburg. He practiced law in Chicago before he moved to St. Augustine. While a bachelor after his first wife died, he threw festive parties in the rented Tovar (Cannonball) House. Hardin died (1923) in his residence at 52 Valencia Street (the Seavey Cottage). His second wife, Amelia McLaughlin Hardin, honored his memory by donating furnishings that completed the newly built Shrine of Nuestra Señora de la Leche (Our Nursing Mother) at Mission Nombre de Dios. Gen. John McAllister Schofield also lived and died at 52 Valencia Street (then called the Union General's House). A Civil War hero, Schofield (West Point 1853) was awarded the Medal of Honor, served as the secretary of war (1868–69), and replaced Gen. Philip Sheridan as commanding general of the U.S. Army (1888–95). He died in 1906, leaving a young wife and young daughter.

(23) González-Alvarez House/Oldest House, First Spanish Period. 14 St. Francis Street

Evidence suggests a Spanish soldier occupied a wood and thatch house on this site in the 1600s. By 1727 there was a two-room coquina house here that was home to Tomás González y Hernández and María Francisca Guevara y Dominguez. He was from Tenerife (Canary Islands), and his wife María was a fourth-generation St. Augustine girl. They raised six children in what is now the first floor of the present Oldest House. After 1763, its British owners, Joseph and Mary Evans Peavett, added the wood second story, fireplace, and coquina kitchen, and at times they ran it as an inn and tavern for troops at St. Francis Barracks across the street. The Peavetts prospered, acquiring property and slaves, but after Joseph died, Mary married a scoundrel who wasted her money, and the house went to auction in 1791. Gerónimo Alvarez bought the house. He came from Asturias, Spain, and was employed as the king's baker at the hospital in 1784. He willed the house to his son, Antonio, who became a prominent citizen and mayor of the city (1833–35), and it stayed in the Alvarez family until 1882. Late in the 1880s, one owner began charging admission to see the Oldest House, a name still in use today. Purchased by the St. Augustine Historical Society and authentically restored, it is a house museum that portrays life during the Spanish, British, U.S. Territorial, and Victorian Periods. It is a National Historic Landmark.

Cross Marine Street and turn left (north) on Avenida Menendez and walk along the seawall promenade with the harbor to your right and post–Civil War winter cottages to your left.

(24) Brooks Villa, 1891. 174 Avenida Menendez

The Moorish villa on the bay was built for the bachelor brothers Charles and Tracy Brooks. Moorish Revival ornamental tile and horseshoe arches reflect the popularity of the style introduced in late 1880s in St. Augustine by Franklin W. Smith at his Villa Zorayda and Casa Monica Hotel. The style also appears at Warden Castle, built by William G. Warden, a Standard Oil associate of Henry Flagler north of the City Gate. It is now Ripley's Believe It or Not! museum. In 1924, the Brooks Villa was owned by Kentucky senator Frederick M. Sackett, the U.S. ambassador to Germany, who left Berlin in 1933, when Franklin D. Roosevelt was inaugurated. He was described as a rich man with ten servants at his Berlin residence in Eric Larson's 2011 best seller *In the Garden of Beasts.*

(25) Bayfront Houses, 1865–1920s. Avenida Menendez

Houses of mixed architectural styles along the riverfront reflect the post–Civil War Victorian and Flagler eras in St. Augustine. After the seawall was constructed (1836–1840s), riverside lots were protected from flooding. Bay Street (now Avenida Menendez) lots were built on and owned or rented by northern winter residents, or by the property owners along Marine Street who extended their colonial houses for views of the bay.

(26) Westcott House, 1886. 146 Avenida Menendez

The Victorian-period house built for Dr. John Westcott is now a bed-and-breakfast inn that extends from Marine Street to Avenida Menendez with tiered porches and water views. Westcott came to St. Augustine from New Jersey to be the surveyor general for the State of Florida. In 1859, he and other men incorporated the St. Johns (Tocoi) Railway to haul freight and passengers from the St. Johns River to the ferry at San Sebastian River west of St Augustine. It had wood rails on which mules pulled cars with calico curtains. Mules were replaced with a wood-fired steam engine that burned holes in the calico curtains and passenger clothing and stopped frequently for passengers to hunt for wood to stoke the engine. William Astor of New York, son of John Jacob Astor, while living on his yacht in St.

Augustine's harbor, bought the railway about 1870; his son William Jr. added iron rails and better locomotives.

(27) Bayfront Marin House, 1887. 142 Avenida Menendez

Bayfront Marin House is a historic bed-and-breakfast complex composed of the colonial **Marin House (9)** and the 1880s Hopkins Cottage. The cottage is named for its first occupants, Charles Floyd Hopkins and Isabella Barksdale Gibbs Hopkins and their newborn son. It was purchased by Capt. Henry Belknap in 1891 and attached to the Marin House. Belknap's wife was a member of the Gardner family of Gardners Bay, New York, where the Belknaps spent summers on Shelter Island and on their yacht, *Magnolia*. In 1911, John T. Campbell bought the Marin-Belknap complex and converted the Marine Street section to apartments (Villas Marin) and the Belknap waterfront section to Bayfront Marin House.

(28) **The Bayfront Inn**, 1960s. 138 Avenida Menendez, between Bridge Street and Bravo Lane; and **Rodríguez Jacinto House**, First Spanish Period

A colonial house belonging to Diego Rodríguez Jacinto in the eighteenth century was rescued in the twentieth century by the Whetstone family and is part of the Bayfront Inn. Rodríguez, born in St. Augustine in 1719, owned the house at 35 Marine Street and its lot sloping to the river in 1763. Bartolome Sintas bought his house at auction in 1791, and Juan José Bousquet, chief surgeon at the Royal Hospital, owned it in 1811 but traded it to José and Anna Sánchez Fernández for a slave. For the next century the house was owned and occupied by free black women: Mariana Dolores (a.k.a. Chloe Ferguson) who died in the 1830s; Lydia Kerr Ferguson (former slave of the Tolomato planter Francis Kerr), known as Old Lidy, who in 1861 was the wealthiest free person of color in the city; and her daughter, Hager Carr (Kerr), who lived in the house from the 1860s until her death in 1899. Later owners include P. E. Carcaba (a native of Oviedo, Spain), who manufactured cigars in St. Augustine; Capt. Seth Perkins while he was the engineer-manager of a company digging the Intracoastal Waterway; Theodore Livesay, a Columbus, Ohio, attorney; and Joseph and Josephine Whetstone in 1944. The Whetstones saved the historic house and incorporated it into the center of the Bayfront Inn.

(29) Pinkham's Wharf (Santa Maria Restaurant), 1910–17. 135 Avenida Menendez

Docks and buildings have extended onto the river since colonial times, including a British-built bathing house (1774), Capo's Bath House (1870–1890s), and the Yacht Club (1873–1890s). Pinkham's Wharf was at one time a cargo boat dock, and a private dock and oyster house known as Pinkham's Wharf or Pinkham's Dock after its owner-builder, William Slade Macy Pinkham, city mayor, state representative, avid yachtsman, and winner of sailing regattas in the bay. His Ocean View Hotel was across the street (1880s) on the site of the Bayfront Inn parking lot.

(30) Marion Motor Lodge, 1960s. 120 Avenida Menendez, between Bravo Lane and Cadiz Street

When the seawall was completed in the 1840s, this site became valuable waterfront property. The wood Hotel Marion was built here and was popular when it was owned by a Swiss immigrant, Henry Mueller, former chef at the Hotel Alcazar. In 1910, he added a fourth story. It was razed in 1962, and the masonry motor lodge was built to accommodate the growing American family passion for traveling by automobile to St. Augustine.

End South of the Plaza Tour B at the city marina where historic ships, pirate and Spanish galleon reproductions, are often on view and offer public tours— or return to the Plaza directly ahead.

7

North of the Plaza Tour

North of the Plaza is the reconstructed area. What is the reconstructed area? Early in the 1900s, St. Augustine's colonial buildings between Cathedral Place and the City Gate were inundated by a rising tide of large brick buildings and a forest of telephone poles and electrical wires. Cars and trucks careened down St. George Street, some hitting balconies. Americans rolled up their 1930s shirtsleeves and launched a plan to save the Oldest City's colonial Spanish and British heritage. The restoration plan was slowed by the Great Depression and World War II, but by the 1970s, north St. George Street was returned to pedestrians, and colonial houses were authentically restored and reconstructed by the State of Florida and private donors.

As you travel through time on this tour, walk into the buildings that have been brought back to life. Once again they are eighteenth-century shops, eateries, taverns, and residences. You will step

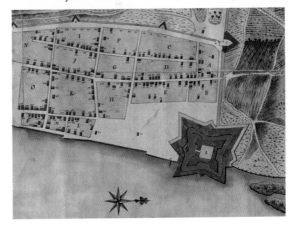

back into their world in amazing never-told-before stories about their colonial owners: the tavern- and shopkeepers, the fifteen-year-old brides, the soldiers and officers, and the rich and poor, enslaved and free. Their large families, deaths at sea, widowhoods, and multiple marriages come to light in their wills, property deeds, records of births and marriages. Their lives and livelihoods are yours to explore—house by house in the reconstructed area and in the Colonial Quarter Living History Museum as well as on the ramparts of the massive stone Castillo de San Marcos.

NORTH OF THE PLAZA TOUR MAP

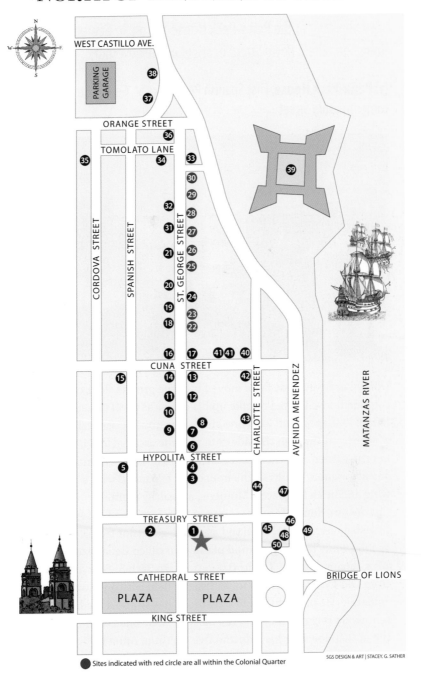

WEST CASTILLO AVE.

PARKING GARAGE

38

37

ORANGE STREET

36

TOMOLATO LANE

34

35

33

30

29

32

28

31

27

21

26

25

20

24

19

23

18

22

16

17

41 41 40

CUNA STREET

15

14

13

42

11

12

9

7

8

43

6

5

HYPOLITA STREET

4

3

44

47

TREASURY STREET

2

1

45

46

48

49

50

CATHEDRAL STREET

PLAZA

PLAZA

KING STREET

BRIDGE OF LIONS

ST. GEORGE STREET

CORDOVA STREET

SPANISH STREET

CHARLOTTE STREET

AVENIDA MENENDEZ

MATANZAS RIVER

● Sites indicated with red circle are all within the Colonial Quarter

SGS DESIGN & ART | STACEY. G. SATHER

Start your tour at the **Peña-Peck House** ★ on St. George Street (long ago called, Royal Street or street of the governor).

(1) **Peña-Peck House**, First Spanish Period. 143 St. George Street, corner Treasury Street

Don Juan Estevan de Peña moved into the ground floor of this coquina house in 1742 to take up his duties as royal treasurer. Large, L-shaped, and with one story, this upper-class residence was entered through the side gate into the arcaded loggia facing the garden. For the next resident, the British lieutenant governor John Moultrie, the house was expanded with a new wing and brick fireplaces. Moultrie, a wealthy planter from Charleston, South Carolina, came to help form the East Florida British government. He served as acting governor from 1771 to 1764 while building a grand plantation called Bella Vista. In 1832, during the U.S. Territorial Period, Dr. Seth S. Peck arrived from Old Lyme, Connecticut, in time to help with a yellow-fever epidemic. He bought the old treasurer's house and added the current wood second story and the balcony with small doors under the jib-windows for his wife and five children. Anna G. Burt, his granddaughter, a longtime occupant (with her pet parrot, Polly), willed it to the City of St. Augustine in 1931. The house was leased by the Woman's Exchange of St. Augustine and restored with funds from the St. Augustine Restoration Foundation, Inc. The Exchange maintains a gift store and offers tours of the 275-year-old house.

A mysterious eighteenth-century building across Treasury Street had an elegantly carved coquina wall (*right*) in the classical Ionic style. Was it the Old Spanish Treasury? By 1877, the beautiful wall was gone.

Bella Vista

Bella Vista was John Moultrie's 2,500-acre plantation on the west bank of the Matanzas River in south St. Augustine. He was educated as a physician in Edinburgh, Scotland; his wife, Eleanor Austin, was the granddaughter of Elias Ball, a wealthy Charleston planter, and the daughter of George Austin, the slave-trader partner of Henry Laurens, two of the richest men in America. Moultrie and his many slaves spent seventeen years building the Palladio-inspired house with classical columns; a ten-acre pleasure garden with a bowling green; a thirty-acre promenade through olive, date, lemon, and peach trees; ponds stocked with fish; and establishing herds of cattle, oxen, and mares and fields of corn. When Florida was retroceded to Spain, Moultrie had to abandon it and evacuate to England, where he expressed his grief in loyalist letters to the British government. In England, his daughter Cecelia married Admiral William Bligh of *Mutiny on the Bounty* fame.

(2) **Joaneda House**,* Second Spanish Period. 57 Treasury Street

This two-hundred-year-old house was built by Juan Joaneda, who fled with the Minorcans to St. Augustine in 1777. He married María Magdalena Marin and made his living fishing, farming, and carpentering. He built his coquina house in 1806 but was forced to sell it to Juan Montes de Oca to pay off his debt. Montes immediately sold it to Nicolas Sánchez de Ortigosa y Espinosa, who was his son-in-law and the owner of 685 acres north of the city adjacent to the cattle ranch of his rich uncle, Don Francisco Xavier Sánchez. In 1798, Nicolas Sánchez married sixteen-year-old María Magdalena Joaneda, Juan's daughter. They raised ten children in this house. A century after Nicolas Sánchez's death, the Montgomery sisters owned the house as their residence, shop, and delightful teahouse with a sunny south-facing loggia, garden, and coquina well. The house was restored in 1976 with a donation from Elizabeth Morley Towers of Jacksonville. During restoration, two small openings discovered at the sides of the chimney suggested gun ports aimed toward the defensive Rosario Line.

(3) Sánchez-Burt House, 1816–29. 105 St. George Street

Traced to Don Manuel García de Fuentes in the First Spanish Period, then to British residents and to José de Landa of Havana in 1784, this property over the years had a number of upper-class owners, including Don Francisco Xavier Sánchez from 1794 until his death in 1807, when it was willed to his biracial daughter, Catalina Rose. She sold the property with a wood house to her aunt, María Antonia Hill, sister of Sánchez's widow, Mary Hill (María del Carmen Hill), who built this large two-story stone house. In 1829, it was bought by Augustus Poujoud, a native of France who had married into the Sánchez family. James Louis Petigru of South Carolina was the owner from 1845 until it was purchased in 1852 by George Burt, a St. Augustine businessman and mayor who married Lucy Rockwell Peck, daughter of Dr. Seth S. Peck (see **Peña-Peck House [1]**). Burt's only surviving child, Anna G. Burt (1850–1931), maintained it as a rental until her estate sold it in 1940 with restrictive covenants to Jacob F. Bryan III, president of Independent Life Insurance Company. When Bryan restored the house and its formal garden as a company mu-

seum and offices, he retained its colonial St. Augustine style combining Spanish and British elements as well as its American central hall stairwell plan. It is currently commercially leased.

(4) Casa del Hidalgo, 1965. Corner St. George and Hypolita Streets

Casa del Hidalgo (house of a Spanish nobleman) was built by Spain to participate in St. Augustine's four-hundredth anniversary celebration of the city's Spanish heritage. It was constructed to showcase Spanish architecture and displays of Spanish arts and crafts. Vice President Lyndon Johnson laid the cornerstone. Sold to the city in 2004, the Spanish-style house is now leased to commercial enterprises.

(5) Fornells House, Second Spanish Period. 62 Spanish Street, corner Hypolita Street

Don Pedro Fornells, of Cuidadela, Minorca, built this coquina house about 1801 on a large lot that had been the kitchen garden of the nearby dragoon (mounted infantry) barracks. When Fornells died unexpectedly in 1807, his estate inventory revealed he had planted 93 orange trees in rows and owned 103 smaller orange trees. His widow, Mariana Tudorina, the former widow of Marcos Andreu, lived in the house until she died in 1820; her estate documents revealed that the house had glass windows and cupboards with glass doors. Burton Masters (originally Maestre), known as Uncle Birtie and the last Minorcan to own the house, operated a restaurant here for thirty years that was said to be the only place in town for real Minorcan food, like shrimp pilau (pronounced "per-lo") and clam chowder (see recipes in section 9). The house was in danger of demolition before the St. Augustine Historical Society bought and restored it in 1952 and sold it with exterior restrictive covenants to protect its history.

This two-hundred-year-old house was tragically destroyed September 25, 2014.

(6) Hispanic Garden, 1965. Corner St. George and Hypolita Streets

This small Spanish plaza was the 1780s vegetable plot and orchard of Father Thomas Hassett, owner of the house immediately north. Earlier, it might have been the "lot of San Patricio," a seventeenth-century chapel. For the city's four-hundredth anniversary, the little plaza was created to be a link to Spain and to Spanish arts and crafts exhibited across the street in the **Casa del Hildalgo (4)** and to Latin American crafts exhibited in the reconstructed **Marin-Hassett House** when it was the Pan American Center **(7)**. The plaza was created with donations from Elizabeth Morley Towers of Jacksonville, Mrs. Alfred I. du Pont, and the Women's Garden Club. Anna Hyatt Huntington donated her bronze sculpture of Queen Isabella of Spain to the City of St. Augustine to stand in the center. Queen Isabella (1474–1504) supported Christopher Columbus's 1492 expedition to the New World. The garden is owned by the St. Augustine Foundation, Inc., at Flagler College.

(7) Marin-Hassett House, 1965–69. 97 St. George Street

Antonia Marin owned a stone house here in 1763, followed by
James Box, the British attorney general, Stephen Haven, and
Francisco Entralgo, before it was bought by Father Thomas
Hassett in 1787. Hassett was a thirty-three-year-old Irish priest
who had recently arrived in the city after completing his studies at the Irish College in Salamanca, Spain, and teaching in
Philadelphia. He suffered a shipwreck on his passage to Florida
and lost all of his possessions. He was parish priest and vicar to
the city's Minorcans and opened his church on the second floor
of the former British Statehouse (where Trinity Church stands
today—see Plaza Walk). Father Hassett set up a free school for
Minorcan children and assisted in the new cathedral plans. His St.
Augustine–style colonial house has wooden window grilles (*rejas*),
a street balcony, side entrance, and a British-style wood addition.
Its reconstruction was made possible by American corporations
doing business in Latin America. For ten years it was the Pan
American Center, displaying regional arts and crafts. Today it is
owned by the St. Augustine Foundation, Inc.

(8) Santoyo House, 1966. 91 St. George Street

Sitting back from the street, reconstructed and owned by the St. Augustine Foundation, Inc., this small house represents the tabby house that in 1763 belonged to Miguel Santoyo, a member of the dragoon regiment. He was the son of Juan de la Rosa Santoyo, a soldier at the Castillo, and Maria Ana Cavallero. In 1756, he married María Maniller, also of St. Augustine, daughter of Luis Maniller and Francisca Escovedo. They raised a large family in this little house that, according to archaeologists, had only two rooms and a dirt or wood floor. It disappeared during the British Period.

(9) Acosta House, 1976. 74–76 St. George Street

Jorge Acosta, born in Corsica, built his house ca. 1803–12 in the Second Spanish Period. He and his wife, Margarita Villalonga, a Minorcan, were children of parents indentured at the Turnbull plantation. Their coquina house served a succession of owners and shopkeepers until it was more than a century old and was replaced by a brick building in 1924. The colonial Acosta house was reconstructed in 1976 by today's owner, St. Augustine Foundation, Inc., with donations from the Versaggi Brothers Foundation. Salvatore Versaggi came from Sicily and made his start in Fernandina pioneering in offshore trawling fleets. He moved to St. Augustine and partnered with his Sicilian brother-in-law, Mike Salvador (Solecito Salvatore), who had formed a shrimping company (1902–6). Together they and their families developed the city's shrimping and trawler boatbuilding business and became leaders in the wholesale shrimp and fish industry from Texas to South America, as well as in supporting St. Augustine's restoration and preservation.

(10) **Villalonga House**, 1972. 72 St. George Street

The Villalonga House is reconstructed to approximate its appearance in the Second Spanish Period, when it was owned by Juan Villalonga of Minorca and his wife, María Acosta, of Corsica. They came to the city with the Minorcans granted asylum in 1777. The Acosta and Villalonga families were related through several marriages. The upper floor of the Villalonga House was a popular venue for more than twenty years for dances and dress balls for free and enslaved men and women. They were hosted in the 1790s by Felipe and Filis Edimboro of Guinea, former slaves who bought their freedom from Don Francisco Xavier Sánchez in 1794. Felipe, a skilled butcher, was an overseer of Sánchez's Diego Plains cattle ranch. Like the Acosta House next door, the Villalonga House is owned by the St. Augustine Foundation, Inc.

(11) Nicolas de Ortega House, 1968. 70 St. George Street

Nicolas de Ortega, the royal armourer, married Laureana de los Reys in St. Augustine in 1736. They raised eight children in their stone house built on this lot about 1740. In his will in 1762, he left the house to his heirs, but Laureana and the children evacuated to Cuba the next year when St. Augustine became the capital of British East Florida. James Scotland, a house carpenter who arrived in the city in 1775, bought the house and described it as having four large rooms, a kitchen, outhouses, and an enclosed yard. When Florida was retroceded to Spain, the heirs of Nicolas and Laureana Ortega reclaimed the family home, but it was sold at auction in 1791 to Sebastián Ortega (no relation to Nicolas), who repaired the sleeping loft, chimneys, and oven. A period of litigation and various owners followed until Don Manuel Fernández Biendicho bought it in 1808 at a public sale. He and his wife were lost at sea in 1813 as they were returning from Havana aboard *Dos Hermanos*. Their heirs sold it to Miguel Andreu, and in the 1830s it was in bad condition. With donations by A. S. Davis and J. E. Davis of Winn-Dixie Stores, the Spanish and British Ortega House architecture was reconstructed by today's owner, the St. Augustine Foundation, Inc.

(12) McHenry House, 1968. 69 St. George Street

Francisco Suarez's house (construction date unknown) was
bought by the British surgeon, George Kemp in 1769. When the
British evacuated, it was bought by William (Guillermo) McHenry,
a carpenter who described it in 1790 as a two-story house of rubble coquina and wood. He was a native of Limerick, Ireland, son of
John and Elizabeth Serle, and the widower of Martha Hackett. In
addition to carpentering, he was a rum and beer merchant in St.
Augustine. His daughter, Isabel, four grandchildren, and a slave
were living with him when he died in 1796. His house has been
reconstructed by Pierre D. Thompson, a local resident and businessman who wanted to contribute to St. Augustine's restoration.
It was his mother's residence before he commercially leased it.

(13) **Esteban Benét House**,* 1965. 65 St. George Street, corner Cuna Street

Like many St. Augustine houses, this one had multiple owners. It was the tabby house of Pedro Zapata, a native of Malaga, Spain, and the St. Augustine girl he married in 1742, Francesca García. They evacuated to Cuba when the British arrived. Pedro Cosifacio, a Corsican who arrived with the Minorcan colony in 1777, bought it in 1779. Later owners were the wig maker, Andres Pacetti, a native of Florence, Italy; Antonio Berti, a smith and tavern keeper; and finally, Esteban Benét in 1805, who rebuilt it with coquina. Born in 1764 in San Felipe, Minorca, Benét arrived in St. Augustine in 1795, married Catalina Hernández, became a ship owner, and was lost at sea in 1812 at age forty-eight. His sixteen-year-old son, Pedro (1796–1870), became head of the family, a successful businessman, and a Minorcan leader known as "King" and "Boss." He married Juana Hernández and had ten children, one of whom was Gen. Stephen Vincent Benét (1827–95), a distinguished West Point graduate and U.S. Army officer, and two other sons who died fighting for the Confederacy. The general's grandsons, Ste-

phen Vincent Benét and William Rose Benét, were both Pulitzer Prize–winning authors—Stephen in 1929 for his epic book-length Civil War poem *John Brown's Body*. The house was reconstructed on its 1740s tabby foundations to match its appearance in old photographs.

(14) Benét Store,* 1965. 62 St. George Street, corner Cuna Street

Pedro Benét operated a store on the first floor of his home until he built this store across the street in 1840. After he died in 1870, the Benét family continued to operate the store for almost fifty years—it was licensed to sell wine, liquors, and "segars." Like the Benét House, the store has been reconstructed on its original foundation and to appearances in old photographs. Pedro Benét is buried in Tolomato Cemetery **(35)** next to his granddaughter, Mary Carmen Benét Baya, who died in 1868 following the

deaths of all her children, only one of whom reached her first birthday, dying at age six. Her grave monument reads, "Erected by the Husband and Father, the last of a Once Happy Family."

(15) **Juan Triay House**, Second Spanish Period. 42 Spanish Street, corner Cuna Street

Antonio Triay built this house in 1806, but it was his cousin Juan Triay who established the family link to the property. Both were born in Cuidadela, Minorca, and came to St. Augustine with the Minorcan exodus from New Smyrna in 1777. Juan married a widow, Juana Ximénes, and they lived here in a house of boards roofed with thatch while he farmed. He acquired a slave, but when he died in 1801, he left his second wife, Antonia Tudorina, an uninhabitable house. Antonio, son of Gabriel Triay, bought the property and built this stone house and held it to his death in 1845. Catalina Sabate Triay, his widow, continued to live in the house. A succession of later owners let it gradually deteriorate to precarious condition, when it was bought by the St. Augustine Historical Society in 1950. It is restored to its Second Spanish Period appearance with rose-colored stucco and repairs made with wood from Henry Flagler's demolished winter residence, Kirkside. The Society sold it (1969) with restrictive covenants to protect its historic exterior.

(16) José Sánchez de Ortigosa House,* 1966. 60 St. George Street

The Sánchez family became one of the colonial city's more wealthy and powerful families with large landholdings north of the city. José Sánchez de Ortigosa y de Giles arrived from Ronda, Spain, in the early 1700s and married eighteen-year-old Juana Theodora Pérez y de Lansarote in January 1714 (daughter of Juan Lorenzo Pérez). Sánchez was a mariner and hero who captured a ship out of Charles Town bound for Hamburg and brought its cargo of much-needed rice to St. Augustine in 1741. He and Juana raised nine children in the stone house built on this site. After their deaths in 1751 and 1761 respectively, their son, José Sánchez de Ortigosa y Pérez, became the listed owner of this house. Another son was Don Francisco Xavier Sánchez, the legendary cattle rancher and landowner. Donations by Edward Ball (trustee of Alfred I. and Jessie du Pont Funds) enabled the reconstruction of the first Ortigosa house, an early 1700s one-story flat-roof house.

Don Francisco Xavier Sánchez, 1736–1807

Francisco Xavier Sánchez, youngest son of José Sánchez de Ortigosa and Juana Theodora Pérez, stayed behind in St. Augustine when the Spanish left in 1763. By the time of his death in 1807, he was one of the richest and most powerful men in the colonial city, a thorn in the side to several governors with his huge contracts for beef and lumber and shipping interests during the British and Second Spanish Periods. His vast holdings included urban houses, nine ranches and plantations (one of which had nine hundred cattle), and several hundred slaves. At his San Diego plantation north of the city, he raised nine children with his biracial consort, María Beatrice de Piedra, and at age fifty-one, he married seventeen-year-old Mary Hill (María del Carmen), born in St. Augustine to Theophilus Hill and Teresa Thomas, and had eleven more children. After Sánchez died, according to his wishes, Mary Hill provided for all his children equally with cash, houses, and slaves.

(17) Sebastián de Oliveros House, 1965. 59 St. George Street, corner Cuna Street

A tabby concrete house was built here by Pedro González in the early 1700s. He came to St. Augustine from Galicia in northern Spain and married Isabel Rodríguez in 1733 and shortly afterward their son, Juan Chrisostomo Gonzáles, was born. They evacuated to Havana when the British arrived, where their twenty-six-year-old son married Juana Montes de Oca, also St. Augustine–born. By 1784, Juana was a widow with five children. She returned to St. Augustine to claim the family property, but it was auctioned to Sebastián de Oliveros (1791), a Corsican mariner and trader who had just arrived in St. Augustine. Within five years he married Catalina Usina, a local Minorcan girl, and rebuilt the house with coquina. In 1804, Sebastián de Oliveros was lost at sea, and his widow sold the house (1815) to a Minorcan mariner, Gaspar Arnau. A donation by L. C. Ringhaver made possible the excavation and reconstruction of the house by its current owner, St. Augustine Foundation, Inc., on the original three-room floor plan.

(18) Paredes-Dodge House,* Second Spanish Period. 54 St. George Street

This two-hundred-year-old house began with the current stone first floor built by Juan Baptista Paredes about 1803. Paredes was a Minorcan sailor married to Margarita Ridavets, also from Minorca. They purchased the lot from María del Carmen Casteñeda, the owner of the house next door (**Rodríguez-Sánchez House [19]**), which she had acquired in 1803 after the death of her husband, Juan Sánchez. With his purchase, Paredes received the right (*arrimo*) to reinforce his north wall against María's south wall and to connect his fireplace to her flue. Later owners added two back rooms, a second story, and two street entrances. James P. Dodge, a jeweler and watchmaker, advertised it as "The Oldest House in America, 1565." Owned in 1934 by the St. Augustine Historical Society, it was stabilized and rented to the Old Curiosity Shop. It was restored by a later owner.

(19) Rodríguez-Sánchez House,* First Spanish Period/Second Spanish Period/U.S. Territorial Period. 52 St. George Street

The north part of this house was built in 1752; the south part in the 1790s; and the wood second story in the 1820s—its south wall and flue are shared with the Paredes-Dodge House next door. Artillery Sergeant Fernando Rodríguez, from Galicia, Spain, lived here in the 1740s in a small wood house that belonged to his wife, María de los Reys, a dowry house inherited from her mother, Lorenza de Salas. In 1752, Rodríguez added the stone addition to the north side, constructed by Master Builder (*Maestro Alarife*) Juan Pérez. The old sergeant outlived his wife and son; he willed his wood and stone house to a neighbor, Antonia de Avero, who left St. Augustine the next year when the British arrived. After the Spanish returned, her house was sold at auction in 1791 to Juan Sánchez, chief master caulker and owner of the **De Meas–Sánchez House (23)** across the street. Sánchez rebuilt Rodríguez's wood section with coquina and added a fireplace in the south wall, the flue and wall that Juan Paredes would have the right to share in 1803. The second story and dormers were added in the U. S. Territorial Period. Listed in the National Register of Historical Places.

(20) Arrivas House,* First Spanish Period/British Period/Second Spanish Period/U.S. Territorial Period. 46 St. George Street

This is one of the oldest houses in the city and was the first St. George Street house restored by the State of Florida. It began as a two-room, one-story coquina house built by Juan de Peñalosa (1641–1723) on the ruins of his late-1600s tabby house after the 1702 British siege. Peñalosa's property passed to his daughter, María Flores, and then to her daughter, Francesca María García de Aceveda Peñalosa, who passed it to her daughter, Ursula de Avero (b. 1723) upon her marriage to Infantry Lieutenant Diego Ripalido of Spain. Ursula's three sisters, Antonia, Alfonsa, and Juana, also married at age fifteen and received Peñalosa dowry property on St. George Street (see **Avero [24]**, **Salcedo [21]**, and **De Hita [25] Houses**). A widow for ten years, Ursula remarried in 1748 and lived with her second husband, Lt. Don Ramundo de Arrivas, in the two-room house and its south-facing loggia until they left for Havana in 1763. When the British left St. Augustine, Ursula's Cuban-born son, Tadeo de Arrivas, came to St. Augustine as her agent to reclaim her property, which she endowed to her daughter, María de Arrivas, upon her betrothal to a Spanish army officer. They married in 1787 and added the second story the next year. An American owner after 1821 added the attic and the wraparound veranda. The house was heated only by its fireplaces, and water was drawn from its shallow-water well in an

enclosed vegetable plot. This centuries-old house has more owner stories: Paul Arnau, the 1860s owner, dismantled and hid the Anastasia Lighthouse lens to hinder Union navigation in 1862. Later the first floor was a meat market, a cigar factory, a luncheonette, and a dress shop. In 1960, it was owned by the State, and its restoration began.

(21) José Salcedo House,* 1962. 42 St. George Street

Follow your nose to the Spanish bakery in the Salcedo House kitchen. Alfonsa de Avero, the eldest Avero daughter, owned the coquina block house and detached kitchen on this site until 1763. (Her sisters Antonia, Ursula, and Juana owned the neighboring Avero, Arrivas, and De Hita Houses.) Captain Andres Rainsford was the British owner. After Spain retroceded Florida in 1783, Don Pedro José Salcedo came from Havana as a captain of artillery at the Castillo de San Marcos and married María Galán (1786) in St. Augustine. Salcedo owned and lived in the house until an arrangement occurred by which the house was rented to the black Haitian revolutionary Gen. Georges Biassou, who occupied it from 1797 until his death in July 1801. Eighty years later, the house was replaced by a wooden dry goods and gasoline-stove store. Alfonsa's and Capt. Salcedo's house, and its detached kitchen, have been reconstructed with coquina blocks (hand cut in 1962) on the original coquina foundations and floor plans.

Haitian Revolutionary, Gen. Georges Biassou, 1741–1801

Born a slave in Haiti, Biassou fought for his freedom in the slave revolt against French planters. As the self-appointed "Viceroy of Conquered Territories," he outranked his aide, Gen. Toussaint L'Ouverture, but when England and Spain declared war on France, Biassou fought with the Spanish and was defeated by L'Ouverture, who allied with the French and became known as the Liberator. Spain ceded its eastern portion of Hispaniola to the French in 1795, and Biassou and his black auxiliaries were expelled from the island. Denied positions in Cuba and Spain, Biassou arrived in St. Augustine in 1797 with his wife and family and twenty-five of his disbanded followers. In St. Augustine as a caudillo, he owned a slave, dressed in fine clothing, and was always at odds with the Spanish governor about his subsidy. He became a Catholic and was given an elaborate burial ceremony in Tolomato Cemetery in 1801.

(22) **Peso de Burgo–Pellicer House**,* 1977 (Bull & Crown Publick House, 2013). 53–55 St. George Street

A British-style wooden double house built here in 1785 and reconstructed in 1977 has been converted to a British Publick House as part of the Colonial Quarter Living History Museum. The original house was jointly owned by José Peso de Burgo and Francisco Pellicer. On the pretext of hunting sea turtles, Pellicer, a carpenter at Andrew Turnbull's New Smyrna indigo plantation, secretly swam and walked to St. Augustine one night in 1777 with Antonio Llambias and Juan Genopoly to tell Governor Patrick Tonyn about the cruelty toward the workers at the plantation and ask for asylum. Pellicer returned to New Smyrna and led a group of Minorcans up the King's Road to give depositions against Turnbull. Within a month, six hundred Minorcans, Italians, and Greeks moved to St. Augustine and freedom from indentured slavery. Of Greek origin, Peso de Burgo (Bapina Patchedebourga) became a prosperous merchant with banking and shipping interests, owner of two slaves, four horses, seven canoes, and a sloop.

Colonial Quarter Living History Museum

Three centuries of colonial life in St. Augustine are exhibited and dramatized in a two-acre interactive attraction designed to be enjoyed by children and adults. Stroll through the museum's journey in time. Experience how Spanish and British colonists lived in their tabby, wood, and coquina homes, with indoor and outdoor cooking, kitchen gardens, and shallow-water wells. Visit the taverns, a boatyard, an iron-smithy, and a gun-smithy that are accurately re-created and brought to life by reenactors. Climb the watchtower for a breathtaking panoramic view of the harbor and city. Entrances to the Colonial Quarter Museum and gift shop are on St. George Street and Castillo Drive. Tickets can be purchased at the museum.

(23) **De Mesa–Sánchez House**,* First Spanish Period/British Period/ Second Spanish Period/U.S. Territorial Period. 43 St. George Street.

Enter this 275-year old house through the Colonial Quarter Museum and see how it changes with the centuries. Antonio de Mesa lived in the first story of this house 275 years ago. Under his tabby floor, archaeologists found Guale Indian burials, thought to be the remains of Castillo construction laborers during 1672–95. Born in Vera Cruz, Mexico, Antonio de Mesa was employed in St. Augustine by the Royal Treasury as a shore guard. He and his wife, Gerónima Santollo, raised seven children in the one-room house, four girls and three boys, cooking and eating in the side patio. The family evacuated to Havana when Spain ceded Florida in 1763, and its British owner, Joseph Stout, the manager of a large Florida plantation, added three rooms to the house, a fireplace, a street entrance, and raised the flat roof. Stout evacuated with the British in 1784, and Juan Sánchez, chief master caulker of the Royal Works, bought the house. He also bought a schooner and profited from trade with Havana and Charleston, enabling him to add the second story to this house and acquire the house across the street in 1791 at auction (see **Rodríguez-Sánchez House [19]**). Sánchez died in 1803 and left the house to his wife, María del Carman Casteñeda, who stayed until Florida became a U.S. territory; she then moved to Havana. After a century of alterations and a make-over as an Old Spanish Inn, it was bought and restored (1966) to its U.S. Territorial appearance with Spanish and British elements carefully researched and preserved, including the pink scored walls—on which a disgruntled resident graffitied the message "pink stinks."

(24) Avero House, First Spanish Period; St. Photios Shrine, 1966. 41 St. George Street

Doña Antonia de Avero (b. 1717) received this property as a dowry from her mother, Francesca María García de Acevedo Peñalosa (wife of Vitoriano de Avero of the Canary Islands), who had received it as a dowry from her mother. Antonia's sisters, Alfonsa (b. 1713), Juana (b. 1715), and Ursula (b. 1723), also had dowry property on St. George Street, and as owners of real property, they were attractive to arriving officers and officials. Antonia twice married prominent men: Joseph Guillen, a Spanish official and merchant; and after ten years as a widow, Joaquín Blanco, *guarda mayor*, official keeper of Castillo provisions. Antonia vacated her house when the British arrived in 1763 and took her family to Cuba. In her house in 1777, Father Pedro Camps reestablished the Church of San Pedro, the church known to the Minorcans in New Smyrna. The Avero property reverted to the Spanish Crown in 1784, and Antonia's son-in-law, Col. Antonio Fernández, dragoon company commander, was granted custody until official title was given to Antonia's heirs in 1802. Many owners later, the

Greek Orthodox Diocese of North America purchased it in 1966 and restored the house to its 1730s appearance with flat roof and clay water spouts. Today the house and its Shrine of St. Photios are dedicated to St. Augustine's Greek settlers. Exhibits, frescoes, and paintings depicting Greek history are open daily to the public. Listed in the National Register of Historic Places.

(25) **De Hita House**,* 1979. 37 St. George Street; and (26) **Bernardo González House**,* 1979. 35 St. George Street

Two mid-eighteenth-century masonry houses are reconstructed and joined together as the Taberna del Caballo (Tavern of the Horse) in the Colonial Quarter Living History Museum. The de Hita property belonged to fifteen-year-old Juana de Avero, the third Avero daughter—it was her dowry upon her betrothal in 1730 to Gerónimo Josef de Hita Salazar, a twenty-six-year-old soldier and one of former Governor Pablo de Hita Salazar's thirty-two grandsons. Her daughter, Francesca de Hita, reclaimed the house after the British Period, but Juana's thatch-roof masonry house was gone, and Francesca planted orange trees to reclaim the land. Juana's house is reconstructed on its original foundation with

roof shingles and Portland cement to meet today's fire codes. The attached Bernardo González House next door has a flat roof and rainspouts that were typically made with cypress or burnt clay to deflect the rainwater away from the door and house walls.

Spanish Flat Roofs

Colonial Spanish flat roofs are not a good idea in Florida's climate, but they were a cultural tradition brought by settlers from Spain's dryer regions like Andalucía. In Spain, people used wood timbers (*vigas*) and woven mats of canes and grass covered with mud mortar to make them watertight. St. Augustine houses may have used pine planks covered with oyster-shell lime mortar that sloped to battlemented (notched) parapets pierced by clay or wood rainspouts.

Spanish Taverns

Spanish taverns were houses identified by signs hanging over the doors with a recognizable picture for those who could not read. They were club-like places open day and night that soldiers, sailors, craftsmen, ships' pilots, and the free black militia frequented for drinks, companionship, news, and gossip. Wine was the favored drink, stored in bottles or pitch-lined barrels, and diluted with water stored in earthenware jars. Tobacco was smoked in clay pipes; cigars were twisted leaves the length of a candle. Taverns were heated in winter by charcoal braziers and lighted by oil lamps, and in summer tavern-goers sat outside under arbors. Tavern keepers (often women) kept drink tallies and payments on a slate—sometimes a plump gopher tortoise was exchanged for a glass of wine.

(27) Pedro de Florencia House,* 1964. 33 St. George Street

Pedro de Florencia, an infantryman, owned a house on this site described as a house of stone in 1763. It is reconstructed as an example of a two-room house under a flat roof owned by an average city resident in the mid-eighteenth century. Modified in 2013 with a retail street entrance, it is now the Colonial Quarter Museum's gift shop.

(28) María Triay House,* 1964. 29 St. George Street

Sebastián de Herrera owned the mid-eighteenth-century stone house that has been reconstructed on its 1700s foundation. Visitors today can experience the house as the Colonial Quarter Spanish Mercado. When archaeologists excavated the foundation, they discovered two rooms and a side patio. Records show that Juan San Salvador, a master armorer, had bought it from the departing British and sold it within several years to Francisco Triay, a member of the Minorcan Triay families who had escaped from servitude at the New Smyrna plantation and were given refuge in St. Augustine in 1777. His widow, María, for whom the house is named, lived here until 1800 with its side entrance opening into the patio. She probably had a sleeping loft under the gable. The house remained in the Triay family until 1834 and disappeared before the turn of the century under a rooming house. Descendants of the Triay families live in St. Augustine today.

(29) Gomez House,* 1971. 27 St. George Street

Lorenzo Gomez, an infantryman, and his wife, Catarina Perdomo, lived in a wood plank house on this site in 1763. Wood buildings did not last long in St. Augustine's climate, where termites, rot, fires, and hurricanes were ever-present dangers. The Gomez House, now part of the Colonial Quarter Museum, is an example of the seventeenth- and eighteenth-century small practical homes built by soldier families. They typically lived in one open room that they divided for multiple uses. Their houses were roofed with palm thatch or cypress shingles hand-split from short logs. Some had lofts, and most had side entrances leading into kitchen gardens and swept yards, where families cooked in summer. They drew water from shallow wells and heated the houses in winter with charcoal braziers. Interior window shutters kept out the cold and rain. Nothing kept out the mosquitoes.

Shallow-Water Wells

Since St. Augustine's water table is close to the surface, early residents could access clear water by digging six feet down and casing a well with a wood barrel. By the 1690s, some wells were lined with stone. On hot, still summer nights, in local folk tradition, it was the practice to put one's head down in wells close to the bayfront, to listen for the distinctive croaking sounds of black drum, a popular eating fish in the area waters.

(30) **Gallegos House**,* 1963. 21 St. George Street

Like the wood Gomez House, this small masonry house (entered from the Colonial Quarter Museum) demonstrates a typical soldier's home. It is the reconstructed house of Juan García Martínez Gallegos and Victoria Escalona, built on her dowry property that she brought to their marriage in 1743. Her house did not survive the British Period, but the lot legally passed to her children. Portions of the earlier tabby foundations exist in today's reconstruction, and they suggest that the large multipurpose one-room open space was used as a sala (living room), bedroom, and winter kitchen. In warm weather, the family used the outside patio for cooking and dining. Off the patio were the garden, shallow-water well, and farmyard chickens that supplemented the family's military subsistence. Like most of St. Augustine's houses, small or large, the Gallegos House was built up to the edge of the street and did not have a street entrance directly into the house unless it was a store or tavern. Before its reconstruction, a large wooden Victorian-era hotel with a tower was cleared from this colonial site.

(31) **Vernacular Wood House**, ca. 1904–10. 30 St. George Street

Across the street from the Colonial Quarter, this turn-of-the-
century wooden building was
initially a tin shop. In 1914 it
was the Sánchez Funeral Parlor,
and in 1934 it was the McCabe
Funeral Home. Today it is alive
with tourists and is a privately
owned retail store.

(32) **Ribera House**,* 1965. 22 St. George Street

Juan de Rivera's (also spelled Ribera) stone house is documented
on Elixio de la Puente's 1764 inventory map. Built decades before
de la Puente's inventory, the historic house and detached kitchen
are reconstructed with coquina blocks based on the floorplans of
the massive 1700s coquina foundations, which were found under
the 1880s Park Hotel when it was torn down. The Ribera House
is that of a well-to-do St. Augustine family of the mid-1700s,
typically entered through a sidewall into a south-facing arcaded
loggia protected from cold north winds. The house is covered with
protective stucco, and the starkness of its white geometric form

is broken only by the func-
tional wood window grilles and
balcony. It is common practice
in Spain and Latin America
to present unadorned, unpre-
tentious exterior walls to the
public, while richly decorating
the private interior spaces. The
detached two-room kitchen
removed smoke, smells, and
fire hazards from the main
house. Both house and kitchen
are leased to retailers.

(33) Old Grist Mill, 1880s. 19 St. George Street

Merchants pursuing St. Augustine tourists began long ago to invent history. Prior to the city's colonial restoration plan, this frame vernacular residence of B. F. Oliveras on St. George Street was stuccoed and scored to look like stone and ornamented with a 1950s waterwheel to advertise it as an old mill.

(34) Genopoly House, circa 1800–1810. 14 St. George Street

The house of Juan Genopoly, a Greek carpenter from Mani, is St. Augustine's oldest wooden structure. Genopoly was one of the leaders of the Minorcan exodus from Andrew Turnbull's oppressive New Smyrna plantation. He converted to the Roman Catholic faith, married Antonia Rosello, a Catholic Minorcan, established a farming and dairy business, acquired three slaves, and constructed his clapboarded frame house. After he died in 1820, the building was continuously repaired for many uses: a tearoom, a gift shop, and a photographer's studio and retail shop. The kitchen building, with its present coquina fireplace and chimney, was added between 1860 and 1888. A 1915 photograph shows the house with a sign that reads "Oldest Frame House." A postcard sold to tourists about then declares that it was built by the Spanish in 1565. In the 1920s, a mythmaking owner advertised it for tourists as the "Oldest School House." Today its sign declares it is "The Oldest Wood School House in the U.S.A." However, as you take a selfie under the sign, know that Voorlezer's House in Historic Richmond Town, New York, is a 1696 wood schoolhouse, a National Historic Landmark that is owned by the Staten Island Historic Society.

(35) Tolomato Cemetery. Cordova Street

Take the narrow Tolomato Lane west until it ends at Cordova Street. On the west side of Cordova is the Tolomato Cemetery, named after the Tolomato Indian village and Franciscan mission that existed here in the First Spanish Period. It had a small stone mission church built by Governor Laureano de Torres y Ayala in the 1690s and dedicated to Nuestra Señora de Guadalupe—its tall tower was round at the top like a half orange. Occasionally, Indians left the village to marry Spanish city residents, and when Spain ceded Florida to the British, town and mission Tolomato Indians evacuated with the Spanish. In 1777, British governor Patrick Tonyn gave the Minorcans permission to bury their dead in the mission ground. A mortuary chapel built in 1853 received the remains of Father Félix Varela, a venerated Cuban priest (see **11, the Cathedral**, in Plaza Walk). Tolomato continued to be a Catholic burial ground until closed in 1884. Today, volunteers are restoring the cemetery and researching history and burial identifications—while the entertaining ghost tours tell their own bewitching stories.

Elizabeth Forrester

Elizabeth Forrester died in 1798 at age sixteen. Her carved vault is the oldest existing one in Tolomato Cemetery, and it tells us she died "after a monumental illness which she bore with true Christian fortitude." Gerald Forrester, her Dublin-born father, had moved his family from Philadelphia to Spanish Florida, perhaps in hope of a cure in the Florida climate, but the deaths of his teenage children continued. Within a few years of her burial, Elizabeth's vault was broken into and all her clothing was stolen, presumably to sell at a thieves' market. The thieves were caught, and Father Miguel O'Reilly was ordered by the governor to post a guard at the cemetery gate.

(36) City Gate and Cubo Line, 1704/1808. North end St. George Street

After the 1702 British attack left the town in ashes, the defensive wall known as the Cubo Line was built to protect the north limits of the city. It was an earth barrier running west from the Castillo de San Marcos to the San Sebastian River. Along its length were wood platforms (redoubts) with cannon, a moat, and a wooden gate to the road running north. The gate was rebuilt with stone in 1808 with pomegranates topping the posts, sentry boxes, and a wood drawbridge over the moat. A section of the Cubo Line excavated in 1938 by the Carnegie Institution of Washington is reconstructed to show its construction of palm-trunk logs, which did not rot like pine.

Women and Tea Save the City Gate

At the end of the 1800s, tree roots were cracking the historic coquina City Gate, and city officials discussed removing it. Elizabeth Dismukes, Annie Woodruff, and Rosalie James dressed themselves in mourning clothes and black veils and served tea beside the City Gate as a daily ritual until they persuaded the city to save this beloved monument.

(37) The Public Burial Ground, 1821–84

Outside the City Gate is the city's oldest Protestant burial ground, locally known as the Public Burial Ground or Huguenot Cemetery or Protestant Cemetery. The first burials occurred in 1821, the year in which Florida became a U.S. territory and a yellow fever epidemic struck the city. The last burials were in 1884. Many house owners mentioned in this guidebook are buried in the historic cemetery that is owned today by the Presbyterian Church.

(38) Visitor Information Center (VIC), 1938. 10 West Castillo Drive

Beyond the cemetery is the Mission-style VIC, one of the last structures in the city to be built with the local coquina. It hosts changing art and history exhibits, and has a gift shop, restrooms, free maps, and information about and tickets to many attractions and sightseeing tours. In the south garden is the Fountain de los Caños, a copy of the original sixteenth-century fountain that is in Avilés, Spain, the birthplace of Pedro Menéndez. Listed in the National Register of Historic Places.

(39) Castillo de San Marcos, First Spanish Period, 1672–95

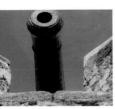

A great event took place in 1672: construction began on the huge stone Castillo de San Marcos, the defensive fortification that was never breached and never surrendered. Its stone construction was in part a response to repetitive pirate raids and Englishmen settling too close for comfort in Charleston in 1670, when St. Augustine's ninth wood fort was falling apart with rot. Thick slabs of coquina shell-stone were quarried on Anastasia Island and rafted to the construction site, where building blocks were cut and mortared in place with lime made by burning oyster shells—and covered with white and red stucco, the colors of the Spanish flag and symbolic of Spanish dominion. It was the work of military engineers, stonecutters, masons, lime burners, and carpenters; Spaniards from Spain and her American colonies, and Africans, free and enslaved, and Indians impressed into service. The quarry master was an Englishman, John Collins (Juan Colens), a Barbados farmer who was captured by the Spanish in 1670 and brought to St. Augustine to work the mortar kilns. He married a local girl, raised a family, and became quarry master. Completed in 1695, the castle is the oldest stone fort in the United States. In 1702, it held the entire city population for fifty days (with livestock) to thwart the British siege, and in 1740 its shell walls shrugged off General Oglethorpe's Georgia cannonballs.

The Castillo was renamed Fort Marion in 1825 after Francis Marion, the Swamp Fox hero of the American Revolution. In Fort Marion were imprisoned Osceola in 1837 and the chiefs of the Cheyenne, Arapaho, Kiowa, Comanche, and Apache Indians in the 1870s and 1880s. Fort Marion was decommissioned in 1900, and President Calvin Coolidge proclaimed it a National Monument in 1924. It was transferred to the National Park Service in 1933, and the Spanish name, Castillo de San Marcos, was restored in 1942.

Osceola

Osceola was Fort Marion's most famous prisoner. He was born in Alabama about 1804. His mother was Polly Copinger, a biracial Creek Indian (granddaughter of James McQueen, a Scottish Highlander); and his father was William Powell, a white trader. In defense of his Indian heritage, he became a leader in the Seminole (Creek) fight against Americans who wanted to remove them from their Florida lands. His anger was also roused by the kidnapping of his wife, Morning Dew, the daughter of an Indian chief and a black slave and the mother of his four children; she was seized and enslaved by a man holding the claim of her mother's former master. On September 9, 1837, during the Second Seminole War, Gen. Thomas S. Jessup seized Osceola's ally Coacoochee (Wildcat) under a flag of truce. A month later, again under a white flag of truce, Gen. Joseph M. Hernández seized Osceola ten miles south of St. Augustine. Coacoochee escaped at night down Fort Marion's walls; Osceola was moved to Fort Moultrie in Charleston, where he died in 1838.

Osceola –
about 1833

a lock of Osceola's hair. The sketch is by
Henrietta Lincoln Daudt... Dr. F...

(40) Silversmith House and Shop,* 1964. 12 Charlotte Street, corner Cuna Street

Two small buildings represent the eighteenth-century shop and residence of a British silversmith, in which he had his tools and workshop, his salesroom and bedroom.

(41) Cerveau House,* ca. 1875; and Haas House,* ca. 1850. 26 and 28 Cuna Street

On Cuna Street are two frame vernacular houses built for the climate—off the ground with porches to catch harbor breezes, and floor-length windows to bring the breezes inside. They are restored to their historic colors and named for longtime residents Blanche Cerveau and Mrs. Rene Benét Haas.

(42) Blacksmith Shop,* 1969. 26 Charlotte Street, corner Cuna Street

A British blacksmith shop was owned in the late eighteenth century by Alexander Skinner. He sold it to David Morran, who returned to England in 1783 and left his wife behind to sell the property. The smithy is reconstructed with British carpentry, adzed timbers, mortise-and-tenon joints, and wrought-iron hardware. The yard once had a pole-and-rail fence to replicate the corral for horseshoeing. An earlier Spanish Royal Blacksmith Shop similarly combined forge and blacksmith's living quarters in the same building.

(43) Luciano Méndez de Herrera House, 1967. 58 Charlotte Street

Named for the Spanish spy who owned the house in 1785–88, the 1700s house was prime merchant real estate close to the harbor. When the British arrived to govern East Florida, Herrera had stayed to manage property sales for the evacuating Spanish, a cover for secretly conveying information to Cuba about British shipping and military matters. His spying activities ended when the Spanish returned, and he bought this house and served the new Spanish governor. When Herrera died in 1788, the house was bought by Miguel Yznardy, a Spanish sea captain engaging in trade between Florida, Havana, Philadelphia, and New York. He owned several properties but sold this house to a free black, Pedro de Cala, the year he became the construction contractor of the new Cathedral (1793–97). Yznardy's biracial daughter, Lucía, married a son of St. Augustine's wealthy cattle rancher Francisco Xavier Sánchez. Southern Bell Telephone and Telegraph Company reconstructed the house in 1967 for its St. Augustine offices; the reconstruction was based on a 1770s description of the stone house having three good rooms and a garret, a kitchen and a garden well fenced, and "in a very public situation." It remains a commercial property to this date.

(44) Charlotte Street view looking south to Plaza, 1880s.

Charlotte Street became the main street for mercantile and shipping businesses after the seawall was built from the Castillo de San Marcos south to the Plaza in about 1700 to hold back the high tides and floods.

(45) Espinosa-Pérez-Sánchez House, First Spanish Period. 110 Charlotte Street, corner Treasury Street, and 44 Avenida Menendez

When Diego de Espinosa died in 1756, his three houses on Charlotte Street were willed to his wife, Josefa de Torres, who in turn transferred one of the houses to her daughter, Josefa de Espinosa, for her dowry upon her marriage to Don Juan de Mata Pérez. The dowry house was the main Espinosa commercial building—a one-story flat tabby-roof house with several street doors, an entryway, and six rooms: shop, storeroom, dining room, parlor, and two bedrooms. In the Second Spanish Period, when it was owned by José Sánchez de Ortigosa y Pérez (the brother of Francisco Xaviera Sánchez) and family, an arcaded loggia facing the harbor was added by a master stonemason, Juan de Poso. It can be seen behind a drive-in bank teller on

Avenida Menendez. The Espinosa, Sánchez, and Pérez families were united by marriages and by their large landholdings and cattle ranches in the Diego Plains north of the city.

(46) Treasury Street. At the north side of the Espinosa-Pérez-Sánchez House, turn east on Treasury toward the river to walk what may be the narrowest street in the country.

(47) Hilton Historic Bayfront, 2007. Avenida Menendez

Where Treasury Street meets Avenida Menendez, the multiple facades of the Hilton line Avenida Menendez to the north, recalling facades that had overlooked the harbor in the colonial period. During excavations prior to construction of the Hilton's underground parking garage, archaeologists found evidence of the colonial foundations and of the three successive Monson hotels that preceded the Hilton, the first built by William Monson (Osmunson, born in St. Augustine in 1815 of Norwegian descent). After it burned in 1914, two more followed, the last being the Monson Motor Lodge, where, on June 18, 1964, a swim-in civil rights protest in the swimming pool was viciously ended by the manager throwing acid in the pool. National headline news carried the story and propelled the civil rights movement forward

to the signing of the 1964 Civil Rights Act by President Lyndon Johnson. In today's Hilton courtyard, find the Monson Motor Lodge's steps that were salvaged during its 2003 demolition. The steps are conserved to commemorate Dr. Martin Luther King Jr.'s visit to the city in June 1964 and his arrest at the Monson.

(48) B. E. Carr House, 1830/1888. 46 Avenida Menendez

Burroughs E. Carr, a successful merchant, built his two-story waterfront house in the 1830s with coquina blocks. It burned in the 1887 fire that struck the Cathedral, but his widow, Sophia Carr, immediately reconstructed it to its same appearance using Henry Flagler's poured-coquina concrete method. An older side-yard coquina arch is an entrance into today's courtyard.

(49) The Seawall

To hold back storm surges and high tides, the Spanish built a stone seawall from the Castillo to the Plaza in about 1700. The British rebuilt it with stone (1774–75), and the Americans extended it (1836–1840s) south of the Plaza to the St. Francis Barracks, a section that has recently been rebuilt twelve feet into the river with an attractive waterfront promenade. Boat basins, bathing houses, docks and a yacht club have been part of the seawall's history. Residents, visitors, and lovers have always been attracted to the seawall to marvel at the dolphins and to view St. Augustine's picturesque harbor where the tall ships anchored in the sixteenth century and presidential yachts in the nineteenth century. Today you can watch a parade of sleek sailing and sportsman's fishing boats passing under the Bridge of Lions.

End your tour at the Seawall, or at the Plaza around the corner, just past **(50)**, Charles F. Hamblen's 1890s **Blenmore**, a Victorian mansion converted to a Mediterranean-style office by D. P. Davis when he began dredging and shaping Anastasia Island in 1926 for Davis Shores, a development similar to Davis Island in Tampa. It came to an end when the Florida Land Boom fizzled and Davis mysteriously fell out the cabin porthole of a cruise ship in the Atlantic Ocean. Today, Hamblen's house is the American Legion Hall.

PART III

❖
❖
❖ St. Augustine Forever

You do not have to be 450 years old to understand what
St. Augustine means to the history and cultural heritage of
the United States. How is the story of the Oldest City told
today and remembered? After learning about the city's
history along the walking tours and about some of the actual
people who contributed to it, here are a few twenty-first-
century highlights, served up in sections 8 and 9, to
help you fully experience the story of St. Augustine.

8

Timekeepers

As early as the 1800s, residents raised concerns about the Ancient City's quaint old structures crumbling. With passing decades, colonial-period houses continued to disappear or were exploited to attract tourists: one owner of the colonial Gaspar Papy House outrageously claimed that it was built by the conquistador Don Toledo for his Indian bride in 1516—a half century before St. Augustine was founded. As a savvy visitor of the twenty-first century, you will find that St. Augustine today is a working city where residents are passionate about times past and present and about historical truths.

Coquina and Clay Clues

Look for walls that have centuries-old coquina exposed where you can see the imbedded shells. Like any great work of art, the devil is in the details for preserving this millennia-old shell-stone, as well as the colonial oyster-shell tabby and Gilded Age fired clay. The Ancient City's craftsmen, experienced in the old methods and the sea-borne materials, are the timekeepers of the city's authenticity. At the Oldest House, the Ximénez-Fatio House, the Llambias House, and the Castillo and Fort Matanzas, for examples, ask about how the original coquina and oyster-shell lime are conserved, repaired, or reconstructed.

West of the Plaza, look at the walls of Henry Flagler's Hotel
Ponce de Leon and Hotel Alcazar and see marks showing that the
coquina concrete layers were poured in place in wood molds. This
experimental technique produced the largest commercial concrete
buildings in America at that time—not to mention what was once
America's largest indoor swimming pool where today you can dine
at the elegant Café Alcazar. Look upward at the exquisite spires of
the Hotel Alcazar and Lightner Museum and read on to learn how
these century-old fired clay works of art are preserved despite
hurricanes and lightning strikes.

The Alcazar Spires

The Hotel Alcazar was designed in the 1880s with numerous tall brick chimneys surmounted by decorative terra-cotta spires, four at each corner and one larger and more decorative spire in the center. Silhouetted against the sky, the spires were unique sculptured objects. Over the years, moisture penetrated the unglazed terra-cotta and rusted the iron armatures, causing them to expand and crack the terra-cotta. Pieces of the spires fell to the sidewalk. Several spires were hit by lightning and demolished. Because they endangered public safety, the spires were removed, but one complete spire of each

design was carefully stored to serve as a template for future restoration. In 1978, the Florida architect Herschel Shepard restored the spires. Duplicating them would have required making copies in terra-cotta approximately 15 percent larger than the surviving spires, for the clay shrinks when it is fired. The cost far exceeded the budget. Tommy White, an expert craftsman from Jacksonville, experimented with fire clay, architectural concrete, and artificial coloring. This mixture did not shrink as it hardened, which made it possible to manufacture accurate copies cast

in latex moulds made from the surviving spires. The iron armatures were replaced with stainless steel, extended as lightning rods, and grounded. Today the spires continue to enhance the Alcazar and St. Augustine's skyline.

Historic Inns and House Museums

If you stay in one of St. Augustine's many fine historic inns or visit house museums, you will meet more timekeepers. The restored historic inns, bed-and-breakfasts, and museums are places where owners proudly express their own sense of the city's heritage, pride of place, and history storytelling. Many of the inns postdate the colonial period, but they are located within the colonial walled town and like the colonial house museums carry the city's historical spirit into the U.S. Territorial, Civil War, and Flagler periods. They are the story of changing times. They are the city of today. You can find photographs and descriptions of historic inns and information on how to make your reservations at www.staugustineinns.com.

Historical Reenactments

Talented reenactors are timekeepers who sustain the colors and sounds of the centuries-old city even as the world around it changes. They close the generation gaps. You will see them dressed in carefully researched handmade period clothing. They are residents who are excited about dramatizing the more famous and infamous historical events in the very places where they happened so long ago. With gusto and gun salvos, they replay the 1565 Spanish landing, pirate attacks, British raids, the closing of the City Gate, and portray the anguish of diverse men and women pulled into the clash of cultures at Fort Mose in the Battle of Bloody Mose.

    Reenactors also enliven our understanding of colonial daily life and trades, from firing the Castillo cannon to tavern keeping to carpentering and forging wrought iron, from soldiering to authentic boatbuilding, gardening, and cooking. For an authentically re-created time-travel experience and to get a sense of the daily goings-on in the lives of the Spanish and British colonists in St. Augustine, visit the Colonial Quarter Living History Museum.

Without the sights and sounds and colors of re-enactments and campfire aromas, St. Augustine's historic streetscape might be just real estate. The reenactors welcome your questions. At www.floridalivinghistory.org you will find a list of reenacting organizations and the dates and times of special events. Join in the fun—and never forget St. Augustine!

9

Heritage Recipes

St. Augustine's chowders and stews have been simmering and perfecting in kettles since the sixteenth century. What colonial cooks had to hunt, fish, and grow for their ingredients, today's cooks are able to purchase and adapt to the heritage recipes handed down from their mothers and their mothers' mothers.

Culture and history bond in the recipes collected for this guidebook. They are from personal interviews and treasured cookbooks in the kitchens of families whose ancestors were colonial residents. Try them and let the aromas take you into the past! The orange wine recipe may be much older than we know.

MISS REBECCA PECK'S ORANGE WINE

Rebecca Peck lived at the historic Peña-Peck House from 1837 until her death in 1910. Miss Peck is said to have often served this wine to Presbyterian ministers, and they always enjoyed several glasses, commenting all the while that it was orange juice and therefore not alcoholic. This handwritten recipe is in the collection of the Peña-Peck House and Woman's Exchange of St. Augustine, Inc.

Historic note: Jessie Fish was making "orange shrub" (a mixture of juice and spirits) on his Anastasia Island plantation in the 1760s and shipping it north.

Dissolve 15 pounds sugar in 5 gallons of soft water. Boil and skim for 20 minutes. Leave to get cold. Add one pint sour orange juice for each gallon of the mixture. Fill keg even full so as to throw off impurities. Every day fill keg with some of the orange juice mixture you have reserved for this purpose. When fermentation nearly ceases, drive in the bung [stopper] in the keg bunghole; or bottle and cork.

ST. AUGUSTINE FRIED SHRIMP

People in Florida did not eat shrimp until a few Italian families immigrated to Fernandina and St. Augustine in the early twentieth century and started the shrimping industry and the construction of shrimp trawlers.

INGREDIENTS

Fresh shrimp, shelled and headed
1 egg per pound of shrimp
Fine cracker meal (buy it or make your own)
Flour
Vegetable oil
Salt and pepper to taste

Peel and dehead shrimp and remove sand sack. Split shrimp along backs without separating, and leave tails on. Rinse and drain shrimp; then, if possible, refrigerate before cooking. Beat eggs and add a little water. Place flour, salt, and pepper in a paper bag and shake to mix. Drop 12 shrimp into the bag one at a time and shake. Remove and shake off excess flour. Dip each shrimp into egg wash and shake to remove excess; then roll in very fine cracker meal. Drop into hot vegetable oil (or lard) and fry, a few at a time. Restaurants use deep fryers, as for French fries. The oil needs to be about 350 degrees or more. Serve with St. Augustine pink sauce (⅔ mayonnaise and ⅓ catsup) with datil pepper sauce. In a pinch, Tabasco will do.

Recipe courtesy Elise Chance via Marsha A. Chance

DATIL PEPPER SAUCE

Datil peppers are generally thought to have been brought to St. Augustine from Spain or Minorca. What is known for sure is that it is a very hot pepper with its own distinct flavor, and has long been a popular addition to traditional St. Augustine dishes. The sauce is traditionally served at mealtime as a relish.

INGREDIENTS

1 gallon ketchup (128 ounces)
6 large onions
3 large bell peppers
3 cloves garlic
4 tbsp. parsley (optional)
3½ cups datils, seeded
3 cups apple cider vinegar
1 cup sugar
1 tbsp. salt
Black pepper to taste

Seed the peppers and chop up the vegetables. Place all into a blender and blend well. Bring all ingredients to a boil in an open pot. Reduce heat and simmer for 4 to 4½ hours. Pour into sterile canning jars and seal with sterile canning lids. [If you want hotter sauce, leave some datil seeds in the sauce. If your skin is sensitive, wear rubber gloves to handle cut peppers, and NEVER touch your face or eyes with datil juice on your hands.]

Recipe courtesy Bud King via Mary Louise Ponce Banta

OLD-FASHIONED ST. AUGUSTINE CHICKEN PILAU (PRONOUNCED "PER-LO")

"Perlo" has long been the most popular local dish and is still made by many St. Augustine residents. It can be made with chicken, shrimp, Minorcan sausage, ham, or anything else you want. Old local cookbooks contain recipes for duck, egg, ripe olive, and "fat hen" pilau. Mary Louise Banta fondly remembers the ham and speckled butter bean pilau of her childhood. The old-fashioned method requires making a vegetable roux, which takes some time.

INGREDIENTS

1 onion, chopped
1 bell pepper, chopped
1 small can of tomatoes
1 package of 6 chicken thighs
1 cup of rice
2 tsp. chopped garlic
2 cups water
1 bay leaf
Thyme, marjoram, basil, allspice, and Worcestershire sauce to taste
1 datil pepper chopped (remove seeds for less heat)
1 package Vigo flavoring and coloring

Fry bell pepper and onion with salt pork or olive oil. Add canned tomatoes and seasonings. Reserve bay leaf and garlic. Cook mixture until it is "dry," stirring often. This takes 1 to 1½ hours. Boil the chicken in salted water with the bay leaf and garlic for 15 minutes. Remove chicken and reserve the broth. Cut chicken into pieces and place in a Dutch oven with the rice, the vegetables, and 2 cups of the reserved broth. Add salt, Vigo, Worcestershire sauce, and datil pepper to taste. Bring to a full boil on top of stove for 4 minutes. Cover and bake in oven for 45 minutes at 350 degrees. Serves six. Serve with datil vinegar.

To make sausage pilau, purchase 1 pound Minorcan sausage, which has datil pepper in it. Fry it in a pan with ¼ cup water. Add another ¼ cup water and let it sit and cool. Cut up sausage and put it back into the water. Make pilau as directed above, but add sausage instead of chicken. Use the sausage broth with water or chicken broth later in the recipe. Minorcan sausage varies in terms of hotness, depending on the peppers used to make it.

Recipe courtesy Mary Louise Ponce Banta

MINORCAN FROMAJARDIS AND CRISPES

Fromajardis (Fromajadas; Fromajadis) are special cheese pastries historically served by Minorcans on Easter eve. On that night young men serenaded outside of the houses, knocking gently on the windows. They sang a hymn that honored the Virgin Mary and other songs, and were rewarded with pastries and Crispes (pronounced "Cros-pays") made from the same pastry.

FROMAJARDIS INGREDIENTS

The Crust	The Filling
6 cups flour	1 lb. sharp cheese, grated
3 tsp. salt	6 eggs
6 tsp. baking powder	2 tbsp. flour
6 tbsp. sugar	2 tbsp. sugar
1 lb. vegetable shortening	4 tsp. baking powder
Pinch nutmeg	
(Any rich pie crust can be used.)	

Prepare the crust as for a pie, rolling it thin. Cut into 5-inch circles. Prepare the filling by mixing all ingredients. Place one tablespoon of filling on one side of the pastry circle and fold the other side over the filling; pinch the sides together with a fork or fingers. Brush top with melted butter and cut a one-inch cross into the top. Bake at 375 degrees until light brown and cheese puffs up through the cross.

CRISPES INGREDIENTS

Use the same pastry to make Crispes. Add a little sugar and a dash of nutmeg and roll out the crust, not too thin. Cut it into circles with a water glass or a saucer and pinch edges up to make a rim. Bake them lightly. Meanwhile make filling.

Crispes Filling Ingredients

1 beaten egg

¾ cup sugar

cinnamon (canela)

butter

Mix filling, adding enough cinnamon to reach a deep cinnamon flavor, and place a spoonful on each crispe along with a dot of butter on top and bake in moderate oven. Option: brush Crispe with egg and put the sugar mixture on top and bake.

Compiled from recipes in *With a Big Lump of Butter*, by Leah S. Lewis (1965); *Food Favorites of St. Augustine*, by Joan Adams Wickham (1973); and *Let's Exchange (Woman's) Recipes*, by the Woman's Exchange of St. Augustine, Inc. (1978).

MINORCAN CLAM CHOWDER

INGREDIENTS

1 bottle (51 oz.) clam juice

1 can (52 oz.) chopped clams

(In the old days, clams were collected from the sand in the edges of saltwater bays. They were opened and cleaned; some were chopped, and some became the broth.)

½ lb. hog jowls or bacon

1 can (26 oz.) Swanson seafood broth (or make your own from shrimp shells, fish, clams, etc.)

1 large onion, diced

1 red bell pepper, diced

1 green bell pepper, diced

2 bay leaves

2 datil peppers or more, diced (remove seeds unless you want it really hot; if you want a little datil flavor and minimal heat, add whole peppers and remove before serving).

2 stalks celery, diced

3 carrots, diced

3 lbs. white potatoes, cut bite-sized or diced

2 tbsp. Old Bay Seasoning

2 large cans diced tomatoes

Fry out the jowls or bacon and remove from pan after fat is rendered. Sauté the onion, peppers, datils, celery, carrots, bay leaves and Old Bay Seasoning in the fat. Add tomatoes, clam juice, and stock and simmer for 2 hours. Add clams and potatoes and cook until the potatoes are tender.

Recipe courtesy Michael Casto

SMOKED MULLET

Mullet are often seen jumping and in schools in St. Augustine's rivers and creeks. In local lore when the mullet were running, shouts of "mullet on the beach" signaled people to lock up their businesses and go fishing. Mullet are not caught on hook and line—they are netted. Historically, large nets were pulled with a boat or with trucks on the beach. Today they are caught with a cast net. Mullet are best either fried when very fresh, or smoked. Residents in the past built smoke-houses—some made out of old stoves with a hole cut in the bottom, or out of old-fashioned refrigerators in which they could hang large fish, such as kingfish, by the tails. Oysters are also good smoked: one Minorcan family interviewed used a cement mixer to wash oysters in the shell.

INGREDIENTS

Butterfly the mullet (do not scale), and leave spines on one side. Season fish with garlic and onion powder, paprika, cayenne pepper, black pepper, seasoned salt, and datil sauce, and arrange them on smoking racks in staggered patterns, not letting them touch each other so smoke can rise between them. Use a thermometer to make sure smoker temperature is around 220 degrees. Smoke fish 6 to 8 hours (rotating racks—those closer to the fire will get more smoke) until fish scales are golden brown and shiny and the meat is not too dry or too moist. Use fingers to eat; serve with cold beer!

Recipe courtesy Clinton Sanders

Buen provecho!

Acknowledgments

Elsbeth Gordon extends a special thank-you to the University Press of Florida, to Meredith Morris-Babb, Catherine-Nevil Parker, Larry Leshan, Dennis Lloyd, and Susan Murray.

Many individuals and institutions, their collections and publications, have made possible this guidebook, its pocket history, and its illustrations. To University of Florida Historic St. Augustine and the St. Augustine Foundation, Inc., thank you for your generous grants supporting this book's publication by the University Press of Florida.

The book is greatly indebted to the following scholars and authors: William R. Adams, Charles W. Arnade, Eugenia Arana, Louis Rafael Arana, Charles Arnade, John Bartram, Beth Rogero Bowen, Amy Turner Bushnell, Verne Elmo Chatelain, Jeannette Thurber Connor, Charles S. Coombs, Light T. Cummins, James G. Cusick, Kathleen Deagan, Michael Gannon, Thomas Graham, Patricia C. Griffin, Carl D. Halbirt, John H. Hann, Karen Harvey, Paul E. Hoffman, Sherry Johnson, Andrew Kerrigan, Joe Knetsch, Jane Landers, Sarah Lawson, Joseph Byrne Lockey, Eugene Lyon, William McGuire, Darcie MacMahon, John K. Mahon, Albert Manucy, Janet Snyder Matthews, Jessica A. May, Jerald T. Milanich, Susan Milbrath, Gregory A. Moore, David Nolan, Zelia Nuttal, Susan R. Parker, Eugenio Ruidías y Caravia, Daniel L. Schafer, Herschel Shepard, Dana Ste. Claire, Robert W. Torchia, Jean Parker Waterbury, Paul Weaver, Brent R. Weisman, and John E. Worth.

Special appreciation is extended to the St. Augustine Historical Society and the Society's Research Library; Flagler College; University of Florida P. K. Yonge Library of Florida History; Florida Master Site File; Historic American Buildings Survey (HABS); Florida Historical Society; State Archives of Florida; National Park Service in St. Augustine and Puerto Rico; the *St. Augustine Record*; Lightner Museum; Florida Museum of Natural History; Historical Archives of the Diocese of St. Augustine; the British Library; British Public Records

Office (PRO) Colonial Office, Kew, England; Ximénez-Fatio House Museum; the City of St. Augustine's preservation and archaeological programs; ACCORD freedom Trail Sites; St. Augustine Archaeological Association; and Woman's Exchange of St. Augustine, Inc.

To Roy Hunt, Janet Matthews, Tom Graham, Herschel Shepard, Dana Ste. Clair, Jenny Wolf, Kathleen Deagan, Robert Harper, Carl Halbirt, Susan Parker, Elizabeth Gessner, Matt Armstrong, Joy Mac-Millan, Carl Halbirt, Nick McAuliff, Janet Jordan, Charles Tingley, Robert F. Nawrocki, Debra Willis, Billy Triay, Elyse Brady, Margo Pope, Julia Vaill Gatlin, Sister Catherine Bitzer, Gifford Waters, George Gardner, and Linda Dixon, thank you for your support and contributions to the book on many personal and professional levels. To Marcia A. Chance, a special thank-you for collecting the heritage recipes and their histories.

The guidebook is a visual work. It could not exist without the images made by St. Augustine's talented artists of the camera and computer: Stacey G. Sather, Jennifer Jordan, Carl Halbirt, Nick McAuliffe, Kenneth M. Barrett Jr., and Matt Armstrong. Thank you, Adam Watson at the State Archives of Florida in Tallahassee, Lawrence Packard, marine artist of Pensacola, Florida, and Larry Leshan who designed this book. A belated thank-you is extended to the Spanish and British cartographers and American photographers of years past.

To Mike, Huntly, and Beth, thank you for your inspiration and fun-filled days in St. Augustine.

Further Reading

America's First Parish: The Cathedral Basilica of Saint Augustine, by Margo C. Pope. Strasbourg Cedex: Éditions du Signe, 2013.

Black Society in Spanish Florida, by Jane Landers. Urbana: University of Illinois Press, 1999.

The Building of the Castillo de San Marcos, by Luis Rafael Arana and Albert Manucy. Fort Washington, Pa.: Eastern National Park and Monument Association, 1977.

The Enterprise of Florida, Pedro Menéndez de Avilés, by Eugene Lyon. Gainesville: University Presses of Florida, 1976.

Flagler's St. Augustine Hotels, by Thomas Graham. Sarasota: Pineapple Press, 2004.

Florida: A Short History, by Michael Gannon. Gainesville: University Press of Florida, 1993.

Florida Indians and the Invasion from Europe, by Jerald T. Milanich. Gainesville: University Press of Florida, 1995.

Florida's Colonial Architectural Heritage, by Elsbeth Gordon. Gainesville: University Press of Florida, 2002.

Fort Mose: Colonial America's Black Fortress of Freedom, by Kathleen Deagan and Darcie MacMahon. Gainesville: University Press of Florida, 1999.

Heart and Soul of Florida, by Elsbeth Gordon. Gainesville: University Press of Florida, 2013.

The History of Florida, edited by Michael Gannon. Gainesville: University Press of Florida, 2013.

The Houses of St. Augustine, by David Nolan. Sarasota: Pineapple Press, 1995.

The Houses of St. Augustine 1565–1821, by Albert Manucy. St. Augustine: St. Augustine Historical Society, 1978, reprinted in cooperation with University Press of Florida.

Lincolnville Sketchbook Journal, by Rosamond Parrish. St. Augustine: South Street Publishing, 2012.

Mullet on the Beach: The Minorcans of Florida 1768–1788, by Patricia C. Griffin. Gainesville: University Press of Florida, 1993.

Mr. Flagler's St. Augustine, by Thomas Graham. Gainesville: University Press of Florida, 2014.

The Oldest City: St. Augustine Saga of Survival, edited by Jean Parker Waterbury. St. Augustine: St. Augustine Historical Society, 1983.

Painter in a Savage Land: The Strange Saga of the First European Artist in North America, by Miles Harvey. New York: Random House, 2008.

Sacred Ground: The Military Cemetery at St. Augustine, by Gregory A. Moore. St. Augustine: Florida National Guard Foundation, 2013.

The Timucua, by Jerald T. Milanich. Cambridge, Mass.: Blackwell, 1996.

Illustration Credits

By page number marked as follows: T=top; B=bottom; M=middle; L=left; R=right

i, 48B, 159, State Archives of Florida, RC06990, City Gate, Stanley J. Horrow, c.1882; ii, 50, ©Stacey G. Sather/SGS Design & Art photograph 2014, view of St. Augustine 2014; iv, v, Library of Congress, 05100, panoramic photograph 1910, Alcazar, Cordova, and Ponce de Leon, Harris Co.; vi, E. Gordon collection, John James Audubon engraving, *Greenshank*; viii, 4T, 15, 16, 36, 37, 44T, State Archives of Florida, RC0-468, Baptista Boazio in Walter Bigges, *A Summarie and True Discovery . . .*, London, 1589; x, Stacey G. Sather/SGS Design & Art map, *Finding St. Augustine*; 1, 39, 125, Museo Naval, Madrid, Elixio de la Puente *Plano de la real fuerza . . .*, 1764; 2, E. Gordon photograph 2014, Bridge Street side entrance; 3T, ©Stacey G. Sather/SGS Design & Art photograph, Spanish Landing Menéndez reenactor; 3B, State Archives of Florida, DG00991, engraving by Theodor de Bry in *Brevis narratio eorum quae in Florida Americae* (part II, *Historia Americae*), 1591, Plate XXXI, *How They Destroy the Enemy's Towns During the Night*; 4R, Stacey G. Sather/SGS Art & Design map, detail; 5T, 175B, Library of Congress, 4a09453, William Henry Jackson photograph 1902, *The Alcazar and Cordova from Ponce de Leon*; 5ML, E. Gordon photograph 2014, Flagler College; 5MR, Jennifer Jordan photograph courtesy Lightner Museum Collection, Hotel Alcazar/Lightner Museum tower; 6T, 88, E. Gordon photograph 2002, Llambias House; 6B, E. Gordon photograph 2014, north St. George Street; 7T, 45T, Janet Goodrich photograph 2001, Castillo de San Marcos; 7R, ©Stacey G. Sather/SGS Design & Art photograph 2013, militia reenactors; 8T, E. Gordon photograph 2014, St. Augustine Lighthouse; 8B, 47T, Collections of the St. Augustine Historical Society, photocopy of conjectural drawing of Fort Mose 1752–63 by Albert Manucy; 9T, E. Gordon collection, Harry Fenn engraving of Fort Matanzas, in William Cullen Bryant, *Picturesque America*, 1872; 9B, 46B, ©Kenneth M. Barrett Jr. photograph 2000, Fort Matanzas; 10, Nick

McAuliffe photograph 2013, Nombre de Dios excavation; 11, 46T, Kenneth M. Barrett Jr. photograph 2012, Nuestra Señora de La Leche Shrine; 12, ©Stacey G. Sather/SGS Design & Art photograph 2014, St. Benedict the Moor Church, Lincolnville; 13, 38, State Archives of Florida, RC03305, Thos Silver 1740 map; 14, E. Gordon, Spanish photograph 2014, colonial Cross of Burgundy flag; 17, E. Gordon photograph 2014, Government House; 18, E. Gordon, mission Nombre de Dios drawing after Hernando de Mestas, ca. 1594; 19T, State Archives of Florida, RC11116, drawing by Mestas, St. Augustine c.1594; 19B, State Archives of Florida, PR09530, Castillo de San Marcos; 21, 89B, E. Gordon drawing, Llambias House, after Stuart Moffett Barnette, Cornell University, Collections of the St. Augustine Historical Society; 22, E. Gordon collection, 1910 postcard, Oldest House; 24, Lawrence Packard drawing 2013, Spanish galleon; 25, State Archives of Florida, DG00962, de Bry in *Brevis narratio*, 1591, *The French sail to the River of May*; 27T, E. Gordon photograph 2014, ship *El Galleon* at St. Augustine marina; 27B, ©Stacey G. Sather/SGS Design & Art photograph, Pedro Menéndez reenactor at helm; 28, 43B, State Archives of Florida, RC00947, photocopy of engraving, Pedro Menéndez; 29, ©Stacey G. Sather/SGS Design & Art photograph, first Thanksgiving foodstuffs; 30T, 44L (detail), State Archives of Florida, DG00971, de Bry in *Brevis narratio*, 1591, *Ceremonies performed by Saturiwa before going on an expedition against the enemy*; 30B, 43T, State Archives of Florida, DG00970, de Bry in *Brevis narratio*, 1591, *Picture of Fort Caroline*; 31, State Archives of Florida, RC07314, Pieter van der Aa's, *Verscheyde Scheeps-Togten Na Florida* . . . 1568, French revenge at Fort San Mateo; 32T, Florida Museum of Natural History, Historical Archaeology Collections, colonial St. Augustine Olive Jar; 32B, State Archives of Florida, DG00993, de Bry in *Brevis narratio*, 1591, *How they declare war*; 34, E. Gordon photograph 2013, giant steel cross with sculpture; 35T, E. Gordon drawing, sixteenth-century town plan; 35B, Prado Museum, Madrid, Phillip II postcards for sale; 40, Collections of the St. Augustine Historical Society, Joseph Purcell, Plan of St. Augustine Town, 1777; 41, E. Gordon conjectural drawing, British Statehouse based on Engineer Rocque's floor plans, St. Augustine Historical Society; 42, Ponce de Leon image, Spanish postage stamp; 44B, 58, Collections of the St. Augustine Historical Society, photocopy, 1594 baptismal record; 45B, 67T, British Library, *Governor's House at St. Augustine, in East Florida, Nov 1764*; 47B, 68, State of Florida Archives, GV002228, Portrait of Gov. James Grant;

48T, 64, Collections of the St. Augustine Historical Society, photocopy, Frances Benjamin Johnston photograph 1937, Renwick-restored Cathedral façade; 49T, 162, State Archives of Florida, PR04934, *Chief Osceola,* 1833; 49B, E. Gordon collection, Hotel Ponce de Leon postcard, after William Henry Jackson photograph 1890s; 52T, Carl Halbirt photograph, ceramic "bacin" c.1805; 52B, Nick McAuliff photograph 2007, city archaeologist and SAAA (St. Augustine Archaeological Association) volunteers; 53, State Archives of Florida, RC05583, *Frank Leslie's Illustrated Newspaper,* 1862; 54, Stacey G. Sather/SGS Design & Art map, Plaza Walk; 55, E. Gordon collection, 1910 postcard, Trinity Episcopal Church; 56, E. Gordon photograph 2014, Florida Heritage House; 57, E. Gordon drawings of parish church—"A" after Boazio, 1588, "B" after Mestas, ca. 1594; 59, E. Gordon photograph 2014, Plaza Building; 60, E. Gordon photograph 2014, Public Market/Slave Market; 61R, Florentine marble lion; 61L, ©Stacey G. Sather/SGS Design & Art, photograph, marble lion Bridge of Lions; 61R, E. Gordon photograph, Florentine marble lion; 62T, E. Gordon photograph 2014, Bank Building; 62B, Collections of the St. Augustine Historical Society, Harry Fenn engraving of Cathedral of St. Augustine bell ringers, in William Cullen Bryant, *Picturesque America,* 1872; 63, E. Gordon photograph 2014, Cathedral of St. Augustine; 65, E. Gordon photograph 2014, Father Félix Varela sculpture; 67MR, E. Gordon photograph 2014, Government House; 69T, State of Florida Archives, N045490, *Portrait of Henry M. Flagler;* 69B, E. Gordon photograph 2014, Flagler College; 70, Courtesy Lightner Museum and Jennifer Jordan, photograph City Hall and Lightner Museum; 71T, Library of Congress, HABS FLA,55-SAUG,44--1, photograph possibly by Prime A. Beaudoin, n.d., *Casa Monica;* 71M, E. Gordon collection, 1910 postcard, Villa Zorayda; 71BL, Library of Congress, 4a03474, William Henry Jackson photograph c. 1880–97, Alcazar Casino swimming pool; 71BR, E. Gordon photograph, Pedro Menéndez statue; 72, E. Gordon photograph 2002, neighborhood south of the Plaza; 74, Stacey G. Sather/SGS Design & Art map, Tour A; 75, ©Stacey G. Sather/ SGS Design & Art photograph 2014, Trinity Episcopal Church; 76, Library of Congress, LC-D4-9103, William Henry Jackson photograph 1902, King Street; 77, E. Gordon photograph 2014, Horruytiner-Lindsley House; 78, E. Gordon photograph 2014, Paredes-Seguí-Macmillan House; 79, E. Gordon photograph 2014, Stanbury Cottage; 80, E. Gordon photograph 2014, Villa Flora; 82, E. Gordon photograph 2014,

Huertos-Canova House/Prince Murat House; 83T, State Archives of Florida, RC28510, *Portrait of Prince Achille Murat*; 83B, E. Gordon photograph 2014, Canova-Dow House; 84, E. Gordon photograph 2014, Bronson Cottage; 85, E. Gordon photograph 2014, Renwick Wall; 86, E. Gordon photograph 2014, Upham Cottage; 87, E. Gordon photograph 2014, García-Dummet House; 89T, Kenneth M. Barrett Jr. photograph 2002, Fernández-Llambias House; 90, E. Gordon photograph 2014, Alexander-ODonovan-OReilly House; 91, E. Gordon photograph 2014, Alexander-Garrido House; 93, E. Gordon photograph 2014, Father Miguel O'Reilly House; 94L, 126, E. Gordon photograph 2014, Castillo de San Marcos, southeast corner and bastion; 94R, E. Gordon photograph 2014, Castillo de San Marcos, cannon in cannon emplacement; 95, E. Gordon photograph 2014, Manuel Solana House; 96TL, 96B, Ximénez-Fatio House courtesy Ximénez-Fatio House Museum Collection; 96MR, Carl Halbirt photograph, Spanish Caravaca Cross; 97T, E. Gordon photograph 2014, Seguí-Kirby Smith House; 97B, State Archives of Florida, RC15639, *Portrait of Confederate General Edmund Kirby Smith, c. 1861–65*; 98, ©Stacey G. Sather/SGS Design & Art photograph, Aviles Street; 99, E. Gordon photograph 2014, William Watson House; 100, Stacey G. Sather/SGS Design & Art map, Tour B; 101, Meserve-Kunhardt Collection, MES21465; Mathew B. Brady photograph c. 1845–49, Gen. William J. Worth; 102, E. Gordon photograph 2014, St. Augustine Art Association; 103, E. Gordon photograph 2014, Victorian-period frame house; 104, E. Gordon photograph 2014, Kenwood Inn; 105B, E. Gordon photograph 2014, Long-Sánchez House; 105T, State Archives of Florida, RC04617, *Portrait of José Simeon Sánchez*; 106, E. Gordon photograph 2014, Marin House; 107T, Collections of the St. Augustine Historical Society, 1907 etching of Puello House, signed G. A. Hoffman (Gustavus Adolphus Hoffman); 107ML, State Archives of Florida, NO32518, *Florida Adjutant General, J. Clifford R. Foster*; 107B, E. Gordon photograph 2014, Puello House; 108, E. Gordon photograph 2014, González-Jones House; 110, E. Gordon photograph 2014, Rovira-Hernáandez House; 111, Library of Congress, LC-USZ62-49297, Charles Fenderich, *Joseph N. Hernandez, First delegate to Congress from the Territory, and Brigadier General of the Militia of Florida*; 112T, Florida News Bureau, Dept. of Commerce, photocopy of drawing by Edward Clifford Bush, St. Francis Barracks 1863; 112B, E. Gordon photograph 2014, St. Francis Barracks; 113TR, Library of Congress, LC-USZ62-101867, *Mrs. Ulysses S. Grant (Julia Dent*

Grant); 113ML, Library of Congress, LC-USZ62-90928, *Ulysses S. Grant*;
113B, E. Gordon photograph 2014, Officer's Quarters; 114, E. Gordon
photograph 2014, National Cemetery; 115, E. Gordon photograph 2014,
post–Civil War African American frame house; 116T, E. Gordon photograph 2014, Tovar House; 116B, E. Gordon collection, Harry Fenn
engraving of Oldest House and Tovar House, in William Cullen Bryant,
Picturesque America, 1872; 117, Meserve-Kunhardt Collection, MES17125,
Mathew B. Brady photograph c. 1860–65, Brigadier General Martin Davis
Hardin; 118E, Gordon photograph 2014, González-Alvarez House/Oldest
House; 119, E. Gordon photograph 2014, Brooks Villa; 120, E. Gordon
photograph 2014, Westcott House; 121, E. Gordon photograph 2014,
Bayfront Marin House; 122, E. Gordon photograph 2014, Bayfront Inn;
123, E. Gordon photograph 2014, ship *El Galleon* at marina; 124T, E.
Gordon photograph 2014, north St. George Street; 124B, Library of
Congress, LC-D4-500157, Detroit Publishing Co., photograph possibly by
William Henry Jackson c. 1900–1920, north St. George Street; 127, Stacey
G. Sather/SGS Design & Art map, North of Plaza Tour; 128, E. Gordon
photograph 2014, Peña-Peck House; 129, State Archives of Florida,
RC08803, Old Spanish Treasury 1870s; 130, E. Gordon photograph 2014,
Joaneda House; 131, E. Gordon photograph 2014, Sánchez-Burt House;
133, E. Gordon photograph 2014, Queen Isabella statue, Hispanic
Garden; 134, E. Gordon photograph 2014, Marin-Hassett House; 135, E.
Gordon photograph 2014, Acosta House; 136, E. Gordon photograph
2014, Villalonga House; 137, E. Gordon photograph 2014, Nicolas Ortega
House; 138, E. Gordon photograph 2014, McHenry House; 139, E. Gordon
photograph 2014, Benét House; 140B, E. Gordon photograph 2014, Benét
Store; 140T, State Archives of Florida, RC19690, *Painted Portrait of Pedro
Benet "King of the Minorcans"*; 141, E. Gordon photograph 2014, Juan
Triay House; 142, E. Gordon photograph 2014, José Sánchez Ortigoza
House; 143, E. Gordon photograph 2014, Sebastián Oliveros House; 144,
E. Gordon photograph 2014, Paredes-Dodge House; 145, E. Gordon
photograph 2014, Rodríguez-Sánchez House; 146, E. Gordon photograph
2014, Arrivas House; 147T, E. Gordon photograph 2014, Salcedo House;
147B, Wickimedia Commons, Juan Georges Biassou, from Juan López
Cancelada, *Vida de J. J. Dessalines,* Mexico, 1806; 148, Courtesy Colonial
Quarter Living History Museum; 149, E. Gordon photograph 2014, De
Mesa-Sánchez House; 150, E. Gordon photograph 2014, Avero House;
151T, E. Gordon photograph 2014, De Hita House; 151B, E. Gordon

photograph 2014, Bernardo González House; 152, E. Gordon photograph
2014, Pedro de Florencia House; 153, E. Gordon photograph 2014, María
Triay House; 154, E. Gordon photograph 2014, Gomez House; 155, E.
Gordon photograph 2014, Gallegos House; 156T, E. Gordon photograph
2014, vernacular frame house; 156B, E. Gordon photograph 2014, Ribera
House; 157, E. Gordon photograph 2014, Genopoly House; 158, E. Gordon
photograph 2014, Tolomato Cemetery; 160, Library of Congress,
LC-D4-17494, Detroit Publishing Co., photograph possibly by William
Henry Jackson c. 1904, Old Huguenot Cemetery; 161T, E. Gordon
photograph 2014, Castillo de San Marcos; 161B, State Archives of Florida,
RC04381, *Comanche Indians Confined at Fort Marion*, 1875; 163T, E.
Gordon photograph 2014, Silversmith House; 163B, E. Gordon photo-
graph 2014, Cerveau and Haas Houses; 164T, E. Gordon photograph
2014, Blacksmith Shop; 164ML, E. Gordon photograph 2014, Luciano de
Herrera House; 165, State Archives of Florida, 2001 photocopy, view of
north Charlotte Street, 1880s; 166T, 166B, E. Gordon photographs 2014,
Espinosa-Pérez-Sánchez House and Sánchez loggia; 167, E. Gordon
photograph 2014, Treasury Street; 168T, E. Gordon photograph 2014,
Historic Hilton Bayfront; 168B, State Archives of Florida, N032468,
Martin Luther King, Jr.; 169, E. Gordon photograph 2014, B. E. Carr
House; 170, Library of Congress, LC-D4-3547, William Henry Jackson
photograph c. 1880–97, *The Sea Wall, St. Augustine*; 171,©Stacey G.
Sather/SGS Design & Art photograph, Pedro Menéndez reenactor; 172,
Library of Congress, HABS FLA,55-SAUG,27—6, Prime A. Beaudoin
photograph 1961, coquina Doric capital, *Rear Arcade Detail - Perez-San-
chez House*; 174, Kenneth M. Barrett Jr. photocopy, Collections of the St.
Augustine Historical Society, Llambias House loggia stone cutters, 950s;
175T, Jennifer Jordan courtesy Lightner Museum Collection, Hotel
Alcazar spires; 177, ©Stacey G. Sather/SGS Design & Art photograph,
militia reenactors; 178, ©Stacey G. Sather/SGS Design & Art photograph,
colonial foodstuffs; 179, ©Stacey G. Sather/SGS Design & Art photograph, colonial kitchen Gallegos House; 180, ©Stacey G. Sather/SGS
Design & Art photograph, foodstuffs, *Buen Provecho*.

Index

ELSBETH "BUFF" GORDON is an architectural historian living in St. Augustine. She is the author of *Florida's Colonial Architectural Heritage* and *Heart and Soul of Florida: Sacred Sites and Historic Architecture.*

Working with Buff Gordon, the Florida Humanities Council is pleased to offer an audio walking tour of several sites presented in *Walking St. Augustine.* Snap the QR code and enjoy!